VEGETABLE SOUP FOR THE SOUL

VEGETABLE SOUP FOR THE SOUL

**The Soul's One-Stop Soup—
From Identity to Eternity**

PRANESHWAR DAS

An imprint of
Srishti Publishers & Distributors

Srishti Publishers & Distributors
A unit of AJR Publishing LLP
212A, Peacock Lane, Shahpur Jat,
New Delhi – 110 049

editorial@srishtipublishers.com

First published in India by Bold,
An imprint of Srishti Publishers & Distributors in 2026

10 9 8 7 6 5 4 3 2 1

This is a work of non-fiction based on the author's experiences and life-learnings. The views expressed in this book are the author's own and are not intended to hurt or disrespect any individual, community, sect or belief system.

The dialogues from the movie *The Matrix* on pp 95-96 are for representation purposes only. It is used under the principles of fair use for commentary/ educational purposes.

Printed and bound in India

Contents

PREFACE

I am a full-time monk who has practised spirituality in India since 1995, nearly 30 years. After completing my engineering degree, I worked for three years at a multinational firm before experiencing my moment of truth and taking a giant leap of faith. I often reflect on this decision, and I truly believe it was one of the best choices I have made in my life. People have frequently asked me what led to my transformation from a young professional to a renounced monk, and my answer is always the same: Knowledge inspires renunciation. No one gives up anything unless they discover something more profound, or rather, the best.

A transformative book struck me deeply, awakening me to reality and providing satisfying answers to my existential questions of life. Questions I have pondered since my childhood. Many of us grapple with these questions at some point in our lives. In 1995, I discovered the works of His Divine Grace A.C. Bhaktivedanta Swami Prabhupada, a spiritual, philosophical, and religious teacher from India. His books are and will always continue to be a source of inspiration to me and millions of genuine seekers around the world. Thus began my long and arduous journey toward perfection. Since then, I have had the fortune of learning and practising under several spiritual masters, including in particular HG Mahaman Prabhuji, a very senior disciple of Srila Prabhupada, a dedicated Vaishnava Guru in ISKCON whose deep devotion, humility, and tireless service have profoundly shaped my spiritual journey; and HH Radhanath Swami Maharaj, a world-renowned American Hindu Gaudiya Vaishnava guru, community-builder, activist, and author.

This book was written over two years in Indore, India, although the conception and ideas behind it are much older. I have long desired to present spirituality in this format. You might wonder about the style of this book, why I chose this style, and how it differs from other spiritual works. The answer is that the ancient books of India—the Vedas, the Bhagavad Gita, the Bhagavata Purana, and the Mahabharata—contain essential truths crucial to human life and also for the benefit of all sentient beings. Unfortunately, a large portion of the educated and academic community of the world remains bereft of this rich treasure of knowledge. Therefore, this book is a humble attempt to build a bridge and present these insights to an intellectual audience in a form that is hopefully acceptable and digestible. Additionally, it serves as a way for me to share the best I have received, as an offering of gratitude to those who transformed my life for the better; nay, best.

I would like to take this opportunity to thank everyone who helped me in writing this book.

Wishing all readers Godspeed.

Praneshwar Das
November 2025

CHAPTER 1

INTRODUCTION

Why Vegetable Soup for the Soul?

There's something uniquely comforting about a bowl of hot soup. It warms you from the inside out. It soothes. It heals. It feels like a gentle embrace in edible form. But why, you may ask, have I chosen vegetable soup for the soul? Why not chicken soup, which many people around the world consider a comfort food? Why specifically vegetable soup?

The answer lies in a simple yet profound truth: if something is to nourish not just the body but also the soul, it must be pure, nonviolent, and aligned with the principles of compassion. Spirituality and unnecessary violence travel in opposite directions. They cannot walk the same path. Violence, especially for the mere satisfaction of the tongue, does not nourish the soul. In fact, it distances us from it. In contrast, a warm bowl of vegetable soup symbolizes peace, healing, and kindness. It is food that harmonizes with the body, the mind, and the soul – all at once.

Soups have always held a special place in my heart. Whenever I am invited to a special meal, I almost always look forward to the soup. They are delicious starters, they can be both sipped and munched, and they create a perfect opening to a satisfying meal. But beyond the taste and texture, soups are low-calorie, filling, and wonderfully easy on the digestion. They help us avoid overeating while still feeling satisfied. Most importantly, soups are known across cultures as the go-to food when one is sick. In those moments, we turn to soup not just for taste, but for healing. Similarly, when our soul is sick or tired, we need nourishment that can revive us from within. That's what this book is meant to offer: simple, digestible wisdom that comforts, heals, and strengthens the soul.

Food is much more than nutrition. Different types of food have a profound impact on our consciousness, our thoughts, our emotions, and even our behavior. Some foods agitate the mind, some make us sluggish, and some help us feel balanced and peaceful. This idea is deeply rooted in the ancient wisdom of India, and we will explore it further in the upcoming chapters. For now, just know this: the kind of food you eat does not just build your body, it shapes your consciousness.

This book, *Vegetable Soup for the Soul*, is a collection of nourishing stories, powerful life lessons, and timeless wisdom meant to holistically heal and energize the body, mind, and soul. You see, these three—the body, the mind, and the soul—are inseparably connected. You cannot truly heal one while ignoring the others. A strong body supports a calm, focused mind. A peaceful mind encourages a healthy body. But even if the body and mind are in perfect condition, and the soul is neglected, we have missed the most essential part of life's journey.

There is a saying: "Sleep does not help when the soul is tired." How true that is! We can rest, we can exercise, we can pamper our bodies with all sorts of luxury, but if the soul is starving, none of it will bring true satisfaction.

Through this book, I hope to create in you a spiritual appetite. Just like soups stimulate hunger for the main course, this book is designed to ignite your hunger for deeper truths, for a spiritual journey, for a genuine search for life's purpose.

But why soup? Why not some grand dessert or an extravagant dish? It's because soup is simple, light, and approachable. You don't need a grand occasion to have soup. Soup meets you where you are. Whether you're celebrating, recovering, or simply pausing in life. And that's how spiritual knowledge should be — not something distant or intimidating, but something you can begin savouring right now.

Just as soup comforts you on a cold day, wisdom comforts you during the storms of life. Soup gently prepares you for the next course, and in the same way, I hope this book gently prepares you for your own deeper exploration of the self, the soul, and the Supreme.

Acquiring Certain Knowledge in the Age of Information Explosion

We live in the Information Age, an era where knowledge is abundant, easily accessible, and just a few clicks away. Google, YouTube, social media, blogs — information is exploding all around us. It's thrilling, but also dangerous. Because not all that glitters is gold. And not all that's available is true.

Especially when it comes to matters of life's purpose, the soul, or spiritual well-being, the internet offers an overwhelming ocean of opinions, half-truths, and sometimes outright misinformation. In the middle of this information storm, how do we find certain knowledge? Knowledge that is not temporary or speculative, but solid, reliable, and timeless.

You see, life is too precious to spend wandering in trial and error. Some errors can be costly, especially when they concern the direction of your life. Imagine boarding a train without knowing whether it will take you to your desired destination — would you take that chance? Probably not. But that's what many people do in life. They follow random sources of information, hoping it will lead them to happiness, only to discover much later that they were on the wrong track.

That's why philosophers have deeply studied how we acquire knowledge. The branch of philosophy that deals with this is called 'Epistemology'. It asks the big question: How do we know what we know?

There are many ways to gain information, but the three primary methods of acquiring knowledge are:

1. *Pratyaksha* (Direct Perception)
2. *Anumana* (Inference)
3. *Shabda* (Hearing from Authority)

The Limitations of Direct Perception

Direct perception means acquiring knowledge through our senses, i.e. sight, hearing, taste, smell, and touch. It's a bit like a courtroom witness saying, "I saw the crime."

But can our senses always be trusted? Sadly, no.

Our senses are imperfect and limited. For example, the sun and the moon appear tiny to our eyes, like small balls in the sky, but in reality, they are gigantic celestial bodies. Optical illusions prove that our eyes can deceive us. Our tongue can mislead us. For instance, if you drink bitter tea after eating a sweet, the tea suddenly tastes sour! Even our ears can't pick up all sounds; we can't hear ultrasonic frequencies like a dog can.

Our senses have a limited range. They cannot perceive everything. Hence, Pratyaksha is not a reliable way to acquire absolute knowledge.

The Uncertainty of Inference

Anumana or inference means deducing something based on patterns and previous experiences. For example, if you see smoke rising from a distant mountain, you infer that there is fire.

Why? Because you've always seen that where there's smoke, there's fire.

Inference is helpful, but it's not foolproof. Weather forecasts are based on inference, but how often do they turn out wrong? They can predict sunshine, but it rains instead. They can predict rain, but the skies remain clear.

Inference can guide us sometimes, but it is not 100% certain. It leaves room for doubt, revision, and error.

The Certainty of Hearing from Authority

This brings us to the most reliable method: Shabda, hearing from a trustworthy authority. This is how children learn most of their knowledge. They trust their parents, their teachers, and their textbooks. Children don't test whether gravity works; they simply accept it when they're taught.

When the authority is reliable, the knowledge passed down is certain.

But the question is: Who is the ultimate authority when it comes to spiritual knowledge? Not everyone can claim that position. It cannot be our social media influencers, nor random self-proclaimed gurus. Even our loving parents cannot always guide us fully in spiritual matters.

True spiritual authority comes from a chain of teachers that traces back to the Supreme Lord. Just like every valuable product comes with a manual from its manufacturer, life too comes with a manual – the Vedas. And there are genuine, time-tested schools of spiritual education. They are the four authentic *sampradayas*, or spiritual universities.

These four sampradayas all trace their wisdom directly to God, passed down carefully through an unbroken chain of teachers, without distortion.

Among these, the Brahma Madhva Gaudiya Sampradaya is especially dear to me, because it carries the teachings of His Divine Grace A.C. Bhaktivedanta Swami Prabhupada, a great spiritual leader who made the treasure of Vedic knowledge accessible to the entire world. His translations, his books, and his practical examples continue to heal souls across continents.

What you will read in this book is based on that timeless knowledge. Not guesswork. Not temporary trends. Not intellectual showmanship. This book is lovingly prepared from the nourishing recipes of the ancient scriptures, especially the Bhagavad Gita and the Srimad Bhagavatam, as revealed by Srila Prabhupada and passed down in their purest form.

The truths you'll find here are simple, clear, and applicable to everyday life. They are like warm soup: easy to digest, comforting, and deeply satisfying.

In this journey, I invite you to pick up your soup bowls, sip gently, savour every spoonful of this vegetable soup of wisdom, and let it nourish your body, mind, and most importantly, your soul.

Bon appétit for the spirit! Let's begin!

CHAPTER 2

ONE SOUL, MANY LIVES, MANY CARRIERS

Certain Knowledge for the Fundamental Questions of Life

A lot of theories surround a few fundamental questions of existence. Scientists have been trying to unravel the mysteries related to these questions for time immemorial. Fundamental existential questions include: What is life? What is the origin of life? What is the evolution of life? What is the origin of the world?

Several theories, each with multiple variations, have been proposed from time to time. Darwin's theory, for example, attempts to explain the evolution of life, while the Big Bang theory, in its various modern versions, seeks to decipher the origins of the universe. Theories are essentially inferences, and as we discussed in the introduction, they provide uncertain knowledge. They could be true, partially true, partially false, or completely false.

We often hear that new scientific research or observations have unveiled truths that differ from current beliefs about particular topics. These updates can feel like Versions 1.1,

10.1, etc. Trial and error have led to immense advancements in science. Science has awarded us unbelievable technology and has made our lives much easier. We are indeed grateful to scientists and technologists for their contributions to medical science, transportation, climate study, food production, shelter, and several other subjects. Science has undoubtedly alleviated suffering in many areas.

However, when it comes to crucial aspects of existence, such as life and death, **we cannot afford conjectures, assumptions, or presumptions of any kind**. We need exact, precise knowledge that answers all questions seamlessly, without inconsistencies. Nothing should be left to speculation; the stakes are too high. There can be no versions of the truth. **What we need is certain knowledge.**

For example, Rene Descartes, the French philosopher and mathematician's first principle states: "Cogito, ergo sum"—"I think, therefore I am"—just three words affirming one's own existence. Descartes argued that the existence of anything else other than myself could potentially be a dream, but in order to dream, "I" must exist. Therefore, my existence is a fact based on this logic. While logic can reveal some truths about life, it cannot explain everything.

A simple example is when someone sees smoke in the distance and infers that there must be a fire. However, there could be several other explanations for the smoke. As we discussed in the introduction, *anumana* (inference) or logical deduction can sometimes lead us astray. **Only *shabda*, or learning through proper authority in a particular field, can provide true insights into the existential queries we face.** Different authorities exist in various fields. One of the foremost authorities on questions about life is the ancient and significant text of wisdom known as the Bhagavad Gita.

Answers on Life from the Bhagavad Gita

Apart from other fundamental topics, the Bhagavad Gita reveals profound truths about life. Just as the smallest unit of matter is thought to be the atom, **the smallest unit of life, according to the Bhagavad Gita, is the "soul"**. The second chapter of the Gita expounds this truth, describing the soul as possessing several attributes that are fundamentally different from those of matter. In a sense, the "soul" is anti-matter. In the terminology of the Gita, a soul is an immortal, conscious, sentient being capable of experiencing pain and pleasure through a body made of matter. In scientific terms, life is synonymous with consciousness, and the Gita states that consciousness is a property of the soul, much like light and heat are properties of fire. **We are that soul—single unique units of life—and like us, there are countless other particles of consciousness in existence.** Stephen Covey, the famous author of the book, *The 7 Habits of Highly Effective People,* supports this truth, stating, "We are not human beings having a spiritual experience. We are spiritual beings having a human experience." We are spiritual sparks of life animating a body that is inert and unconscious matter.

Yes, I Know that We are Not These Bodies, So What?

We have heard this before: we are not these bodies, but spirit souls. However, it is one thing to know something and quite another to fully realize it. To truly understand and internalize a truth or a fact is to live and experience it. Hearing about fire's ability to burn is different from actually feeling its heat. Why, then, should we go through the effort of this scrutiny? Why bother? There are countless things to do, and time is always a scarce commodity. However, there are significant reasons to invest our time and energy in understanding the soul and related concepts. **The primary reason is to realize one's true potential as a living entity.** The potential of the soul is unimaginable as opposed to the body, which is merely dead matter. This potential is accessible to every soul in existence. Enquiry into important matters never hurts. Science has advanced in various fields because someone asked questions. Just as the great scientist Isaac Newton enquired why an apple falls down and discovered the law of gravitation, we, too, must ask questions to uncover truths. So, let's ask some questions on the smallest unit of life, of consciousness – the soul.

Characteristics of the Soul

What are some inherent characteristics of the soul? The Bhagavad Gita reveals several. Unlike the body, the soul is imperishable and cannot be killed, harmed by any weapon, burnt by fire, or drowned in water. **The primary symptom of the soul is consciousness, which radiates throughout the body, like a lamp spreads its light in a room.** A person experiences pain and pleasure due to this consciousness; something we encounter daily. For example, the joy we feel when watching a beautiful sunrise by the ocean is a conscious experience that a robot, equipped with metallic eyes, cameras, and sensory devices, cannot replicate. While a robot may outperform humans in many tasks, it lacks the property of intentionality. Anyone with a bit of curiosity and logic can discern the difference between living beings and inanimate matter.

Is there Any Proof for the Existence of the Soul?

Wait! A thought arises: What is the proof of the soul and its characteristics? Who has actually seen the soul? It's perfectly fine to have doubts. Nothing should be either accepted or rejected blindly. Arjuna, our hero in the Bhagavad Gita, placed several doubts before Lord Krishna and patiently listened to his answers. Just as it is important to question our beliefs, we should also be open to the possibility of accepting what we doubt.

Why is this important? It is so because much of what we know comes from what we've heard from someone or read somewhere, often without thorough analysis. **The greatest evidence for the existence of the soul is our experience of the continuous stream of consciousness that we call life.** Life flows seamlessly, like a stream of water, without even the tiniest break. We, the soul, are the observers, the conscious sentient experiencers of life. This foundational truth is presented as the first lesson in the Bhagavad Gita, emphasizing the soul as a fundamental reality upon which all aspects of life and death are built.

Regarding the notion of needing to see the soul to believe in it, there are numerous subtle objects that are beyond our sensory perception, such as X-rays, electrons, radiation, etc. Science teaches us that our eyes can only perceive what is known as the "visible spectrum", which represents a tiny fraction of the electromagnetic spectrum. This range of wavelengths, called visible light, does not encompass the ultraviolet and infrared ranges. **Similar to these invisible wavelengths, the soul is also very subtle and cannot be perceived through our senses.**

Discover Your True Self

According to the Bhagavad Gita, you are not merely the body you see in the mirror every day. Your identity does not change, even as the external body, which is a mere carrier of the soul, transforms from a brand-new, tiny baby body to an old invalid body. Feelings, emotions, and preferences might change, but we agree that the essence of who we are remains constant. The body changes, but the soul remains unaltered.

The Bhagavad Gita further reveals the science of transmigration, describing how the soul moves from one carrier to another. The soul is immortal, while the body is temporary and not truly alive. The soul transmigrates from one body to another, just like a person moves from one apartment to another when the apartment becomes old or is broken. When the soul leaves the body, the phenomenon is termed as death; when the soul enters a new body, it is called rebirth. Thus, the cycle of birth, death, and rebirth perpetuates, with ageing and illness in between... until we take action to break this cycle. This is encapsulated in the title "One Soul, Many Lives, Many Carriers". **The beauty is that it is we who choose our next carrier.** At the time of death, two key factors—our desires and what we deserve—determine our next embodiment. In other words, our wishes and karmic reactions (reactions to actions in this life) shape the new form we will take. Every carrier has a beginning, a middle, and an end.

One Soul, Millions of Carriers

How many different types of carriers exist? According to ancient Vedic texts like the *Padma Purana*, **there are 84,00,000 types of carriers.** This includes nine lakh types of aquatic beings (*Jalaja nava lakshani*), twenty lakh types of trees (*Sthavara laksha vimsati*), eleven lakh types of insects (*Krimayo rudra sankhyakah*), ten lakh types of birds (*Paksinam dasa lakshanam*), thirty lakh types of beasts (*Trimsal lakshani pasavah*), and **last but not the least, four lakh types of human-like beings (*catur lakshani manavah*).**

Why are there so many types of carriers? Each type provides unique opportunities for a soul to fulfill distinct desires. For example, if one wishes to fly, the bird carrier exists; if one loves water, aquatic carriers are available; and for those with a passion for eating, a hog carrier is present. There are millions of such permutations and combinations of desires, which is why so many carriers exist, akin to how three primary colours can create millions of different shades.

The Human Carrier - The Rarest of them All

An invaluable insight from ancient scriptures is that after passing through 8 million different types of carriers, a soul finally obtains the first human carrier, a human body. The human carrier is unique in that it possesses an advanced awareness of being alive. The other 8 million carriers represent a spectrum of increasing consciousness. Different levels of consciousness exist among varying carriers. Just as the light of a lamp can be muted by shades, the soul's consciousness can be obscured in this world by different types of bodies of which there are 84,00,000 types. These categories are as follows:

1. *Avrita-chetana* (covered consciousness)
   – Trees, plants, creepers, mountains, etc.

2. *Sankuchita-chetana* (contracted or shrunken consciousness)
   – Aquatics, birds, beasts, etc.

3. *Mukulita-chetana* (budding consciousness)
   – Human beings only

4. *Vikasita-chetana* (blossoming consciousness)
   – Human beings only

5. *Purna-vikasita-chetana* (completely blossomed consciousness)
   – Human beings only

The scriptures explain these various levels of consciousness. Souls that are in the *avrita* or "covered consciousness" stage are trees. Trees and plants are almost inert. **Trees have life as per the scriptures, and this was proven even by Indian scientist Jagdish Chandra Bose.** However, trees lack a complex nervous system and experience significantly less pain when harmed compared to other living beings. This diminished capacity for pain correlates with their covered consciousness. The more the consciousness is covered, the less pain one feels. Other living entities, such as worms, insects, and animals, possess *sankuchita* or "shrunken consciousness". Their consciousness is not as much covered as that of plants or trees, but it is not yet fully developed.

Human beings have *mukulita* 'or "budding consciousnesses". Just as a bud appears to be underdeveloped yet holds the potential to bloom into a flower, humans, too, possess a budding consciousness and an inherent capability for developing it, potentially reaching the point of knowing and realizing God.

The *Vedanta Sutra* opens with the aphorism "*Athato Brahma Jignasa*", meaning **"Now, after attaining this human body, enquire about the Absolute Truth."** Thus, the Vedic scriptures hold the human form in high regard and consider it to be the most elevated and sacred species. When a human engages in "*Brahma Jignasa*", or sincere enquiry, regarding the Absolute Truth, their budding underdeveloped consciousness begins to evolve. This is the 'blossoming' state of consciousness. When, as a result of their enquiry, they practise Yoga or a regulated spiritual discipline, their consciousness continues to develop, ultimately leading to the complete realization of God, signifying the 'fully blossomed state of consciousness'.

Attaining a human body follows a lengthy journey through 8.4 million lower species. Gradually, each soul evolves through various stages of consciousness: covered, shrunken, and budding. At the budding stage, the soul has the chance to fully develop its spiritual consciousness and awaken its relationship with God, the Supreme Being. Should the soul neglect this opportunity, it may undergo transmigration back through the covered, shrunken, and budding stages.

The purpose of Yoga is for a soul in a human body to achieve the fully blossomed state of consciousness. One might wonder about the benefits of reaching this *purnavikasita* or "fully blossomed" state of consciousness. The scriptures explain that this is the soul's natural state. The *Vedanta Sutra* says: "*Anandamayo Abhyasat*", meaning, the Supreme Lord is full of joy, and the **soul, being a part and parcel of God, also embodies joy in its natural uncovered state**. However, as soon as there is a covering of any level, the soul's natural joyous state is obscured by "*nirananda*" or unhappiness or suffering, which is characteristic of the material condition. The purpose of Yoga, therefore, is to remove this covering of the material body, liberating the soul from suffering and restoring it to a state of everlasting, ever-increasing joy.

CHAPTER 3

RESOLVING THE IDENTITY CRISIS - WHO AM I?

Does this Question Matter?

This profound question is significant for every single human being. In various ways—sometimes positively, sometimes negatively—individuals grapple with their identities. Some people often feel content with who they are, while others may carry guilt related to their sense of self. Over time, perceptions and understandings of oneself evolve and mature. Individuals become more aware of their strengths and weaknesses, fears, capabilities, tendencies, likes, and dislikes. As they grow, they may reflect on their past actions, recalling both admirable decisions and regrettable mistakes. Many contemplate how they would change their lives if given the chance to relive them, wishing to avoid previous errors or perform better deeds.

Who Am I Really?

Many times in life, we are faced with the deep, unsettling question: **Who am I, really?** This confusion often arises when we reflect on our occupation, relationships, sexual orientation, personal preferences, and life goals. We may feel certain about our identity at one point, only to experience events that shatter that clarity and plunge us back into doubt. This inner search can continue for a lifetime, sometimes remaining unresolved even until death. However, there is hope. If we sincerely seek, ask the right questions, and approach the right sources, we may eventually discover the truth of who we truly are.

Benefits of Knowing Our True Identity

Knowing the answer to the question "Who am I?" allows us to align our work, lifestyle, dietary choices, and other requirements in a particular way because the evident truth is that each one of us is unique in both gross and subtle ways. We are distinctive to the last possible extent. The good news is that even if there may be thousands of others in the same occupation as we are, no one can perform our work the way we understand our field, face challenges, or apply our expertise. **Just as no two fingerprints are the same—not even among identical twins—no one is truly identical**. Therefore, our choices and requirements are also unique. Understanding the answer to this question helps us live a more fulfilling life in personal sphere, professional arena, and in our relationships. Often, we imitate our role models, trying to be something we are not, rather than striving to become the best version of ourselves.

Another significant benefit of knowing oneself is that it imparts a sense of purpose. Since each person is unique, our purposes or goals in life are also different. Knowing and working towards one's purpose makes life more meaningful. This focus allows us to remain happy and steadfast even in the face of difficulties. Without goals, life can feel chaotic, like 22 players running aimlessly on a football field with one ball but no goalposts, or boarding a train without any destination in mind. Quite senseless, as we would all agree. Therefore, it is essential to have a purpose and set goals.

By accepting one's identity, one develops goals in life and then lives a lifestyle based on those goals. In the Bhagavad Gita, Lord Krishna emphasizes that one should perform their own occupational work and not take up someone else's occupation, thinking it would be easier. He also says that one's work should align with their nature, inclinations, and capabilities. However, there are two identities discussed in the Gita: the **temporary material identity of the carrier and the eternal spiritual identity of the soul.** The material identity keeps changing with every birth, while the spiritual identity remains intact and unchanging. So, there is a material "us" which is a temporary identity and a spiritual "us" which is an eternal, never-changing identity.

The material identity is based on the soul's connection with different types of matter. There are primarily three types of matter described in the Bhagavad Gita - *Sattvic, Rajasic,* and *Tamasic,* collectively referred to as the *Gunas* or Modes of Nature. Just as the three primary colours—red, blue, and yellow—can combine in various ways to create millions of distinct shades, these three *gunas* mix in countless permutations and combinations to form the infinite varieties of material experiences and personalities we see in the world. Each individual soul, by its past desires, activities, and impressions, becomes connected to a unique blend of these *gunas*, which then determines the type of body, mind, and even life circumstances it acquires in the material world.

This explains why no two bodies are exactly the same, even when they seem identical externally. Even identical twins, who may appear alike, are fundamentally different on subtle levels. Although they share genetic material, their DNA is not a perfect match; there are always minute differences. Their fingerprints differ, their facial structures may show variations over time, and more importantly, their psychological make-up—their preferences, attractions, repulsions, talents, aspirations, and life purposes—can be distinctly different. One twin may be naturally inclined towards creative arts, while the other may feel drawn to scientific exploration. One may be calm and introspective, while the other is energetic and extroverted. This diversity arises from the subtle impressions or *vasanas* carried by the soul, which shape its unique interaction with the modes of nature.

It is not simply genetics or environment that makes each person unique; it is this karmic journey of the soul, its stored desires and accumulated impressions across countless lifetimes, that influences which particular combination of the *gunas* will manifest in any given life. Chapter 14 of the Bhagavad Gita explains that those who are influenced predominantly by *Sattva Guna* are drawn to purity, knowledge, and happiness. Those dominated by *Rajo Guna* are driven by passion, activity, and ambition; whereas those under the influence of *Tamo Guna* are characterized by inertia, ignorance, and confusion. However, no soul is exclusively governed by just one mode; rather, all three modes are always present in varying degrees, and their interaction creates the complex and dynamic personalities we see around us.

The material world is, in fact, a vast, intricate tapestry woven from these three *gunas.* The uniqueness of every individual is a testimony to this complex mixing of *gunas.* Even when people grow up in the same family, receive the same education, and live in similar conditions, they develop distinctly different tendencies and life goals. This is because the soul's connection to the *gunas* is deeply personal and uniquely tailored by its own history of desires and actions. Ultimately, the modes of nature bind the soul to material existence, but through the cultivation of transcendental knowledge and devotional service, as taught in the Bhagavad Gita, one can rise beyond these modes and rediscover their original, pure spiritual identity beyond the material coverings.

Just Knowing I Am Not this Body but a Spiritual Soul is Not Sufficient

Just as material identity has many aspects, such as a name, parents' names, family, occupation, place of residence, phone numbers, different IDs, bank accounts etc., spiritual identity, too, has several aspects, including a name, form, residence, service, etc. Just like simply knowing the name of a person will not reveal their complete identity, merely knowing that one is a soul is not sufficient for establishing a complete spiritual identity. **Spiritual identity is revealed to the soul in an advanced state of spiritual awareness.**

Secret Knowledge about Our Personality in the Bhagavad Gita

Many invaluable secrets pertaining to the soul are revealed in the Gita. Knowing and understanding these secrets can transform one's life for the better. One of them is that the soul, while in this world, is enveloped by two coverings—a subtle body and a gross body, akin to software and hardware, respectively in a computer. The subtle body comprises the mind, intelligence, and false ego, while the gross visible body is made up of the five elements: earth, water, fire, air, and sky. The subtle body cannot be perceived by the gross senses. In other words, we cannot see, touch, taste, smell, or hear the mind, intelligence, and false ego; whereas the gross body is visible and can be perceived by the senses. The subtle body can only be experienced, and so can the soul.

We are Neither the Subtle Body Nor the Gross Body We Perceive in the Mirror Everyday

There is a Vedic injunction: "*Asango ayam purushah*", meaning the soul has absolutely no connection with the subtle and gross body. Even though the soul identifies itself with matter, it does not mix with it, just like oil and water do not mix with each other. An example in this regard is rain water. When rain water is coming down, it is pure, pristine, and transparent. When it falls down, it mixes with mud and becomes muddy water. It seems as if the water has taken on the properties of the mud. However, we all know that through the scientific process of distillation, we can recover pure water from the muddy water. This is possible only because the water never mixed with the mud; it only mixed superficially and was always pure. Similarly, "*asango ayam purushah*" means the soul is always pure, and whatever contamination (mud) there is in our thoughts, words, and actions is in the subtle and gross body.

We are NOT What We Think, Speak, or Act

Another significant lesson we can learn from this is that our actual and permanent identity is not determined by what we think, say, or how we act. We are not what our subtle and gross bodies are. In muddy water, the water is not the mud; it is separate from the mud. There is much confusion about identifying oneself. Generally, people tend to identify with their gross bodies as belonging to a certain place, having a certain gender, occupation, etc. On a subtle level, they associate with their thoughts. When one identifies with the mind, their identity keeps changing with the thoughts, likes, and dislikes of the mind over time—much like muddy water changes colour or composition when it comes in contact with other types of mud. One should bear in mind, however, that irrespective of the changes happening in the muddy water, the water itself remains unaffected and separate; it **does not change. Similarly, we, the soul, do not change. Our actual permanent identity, which is the identity of the soul, never changes.**

The Question Remains - Who Am I?

Unfortunately, this question is not addressed in any school, college, or university in the entire world. Modern education neglects this most important subject matter and focuses solely on earning money and enjoying life. The result is that we are neglecting the needs of the bird in the cage, while merely polishing the cage itself. The needs of the cage and the bird are different, just as the needs of the gross body, subtle body, and soul are distinct. Each one of them needs to be catered to. A car and its driver have different needs. The car may run on petrol, but the driver cannot be satisfied with drinking petrol. Thus, while we may appear sound externally—our body may be healthy, and our mind may be active—our soul, the real "us", may actually be impoverished.

The first step—understanding who I am not—is answered in the Gita. I am NOT what my body is. I am NOT my mind. I am NOT what I think, say, or act. **I am a pure and pristine sentient being; the terminology used in the Gita is "soul".** Knowing this and working towards its realization is what is called self-realization. However, just as pure rain water becomes muddy when it comes in contact with mud, our original pure consciousness becomes contaminated when we or the soul come in touch with matter. Depending on the soul's association with varied combinations of the three *gunas* or modes, different types of consciousness are formed. The good news is that just as one can recover pure water through distillation, **one can purify oneself through the process of Yoga, regardless of one's current situation.**

Not knowing one's real identity, or forgetting it altogether, amounts to a kind of amnesia. This amnesia is like a disease that requires treatment. If one not only forgets who they are, but also believes themselves to be someone else, the disease is even more severe. Although many of us are interested in selfies, the reality is that we often do not know our true spiritual "self".

Another compelling reason for self-realization is that the potential of the gross body, subtle body, and soul are all different. The subtle body has greater potential than the gross body, while the spiritual body, or soul, possesses even more power than both. **This potential can be unlocked when one recognizes their spiritual identity.**

As discussed earlier, just as the body has multiple aspects of identity, the soul has various facets as well. In Chapter 15, Verse 7 of the Bhagavad Gita, Lord Krishna reveals a crucial aspect of the soul's identity: *"Mamaivamsa jiva loke"*, meaning "the souls in this world are My eternal fragments". Thus, the soul is a God particle—similar in quality to God, but not in quantity. If God is the fire, then the soul is a spark from that fire, a spark of life. The *Svetasvatara Upanishad* describes the soul as being ten-thousandth the size of the tip of a hair on one's head. The soul, it says, is located in the region of the heart, from where it animates the entire body.

The soul is eternal and, therefore, should have an eternal function. What is the eternal function of the soul? Just as a hand serves the whole body, the soul is meant to serve the Supersoul, or God. **This is the eternal identity of the soul. This understanding of the soul as fundamentally linked to God resolves the identity crisis permanently.**

CHAPTER 4

THE INEVITABLE SEARCH FOR HAPPINESS

What Actually is Happiness?

Happiness is often defined as "a positive and pleasant emotion, ranging from contentment to intense joy". In the same breath, it says, "As with any emotion, the precise definition of happiness has been a perennial debate in philosophy." So, what exactly is happiness? This question invites philosophical discussion.

Is the emotion I feel when I savour my excellently cooked favourite food after a long time happiness? Or is it the calm and serene feeling of watching a sunrise on an ocean beach? Perhaps it is the state of mind one experiences after achieving a significant life goal following a long struggle. Alternatively, is it the deep contentment that comes from leading a life filled with achievements and contributing to the welfare of others? All these undoubtedly embody happiness, contrasting sharply with moments of sorrow—a negative and unpleasant emotion that no one desires.

The Inevitable Search for Happiness by All Living Beings

One of the undeniable truths of life is that **every living being—whether human, animal, bird, insect, or even plant—is always engaged in an unending search for happiness, while simultaneously striving to avoid suffering.** This pursuit is not a one-time endeavour, but a continuous, moment-to-moment quest that underpins the entire cycle of existence. Whether consciously or unconsciously, every thought, decision, word, and action is fundamentally aimed at achieving one simple goal: to experience happiness and escape sorrow.

If we carefully analyze the motivations behind our actions, we will find that they inevitably trace back to two core objectives: maximizing happiness and minimizing suffering. This holds true across all species and levels of consciousness. For example, a child cries when uncomfortable or unhappy and stops once happiness is restored. A bird searches tirelessly for food, not just for survival but to satisfy its hunger—a form of physical happiness. Even a tree bends towards sunlight to fulfill its innate tendency to thrive and grow, seeking its natural condition of well-being.

Interestingly, no matter how much effort we invest in this pursuit, we seem unable to achieve these goals fully and permanently. Despite advancements in science, technology, medicine, relationships, and social structures, human beings continue to grapple with deep dissatisfaction and emotional turmoil. If we could completely fulfill our search for happiness, the journey would cease, and we would rest contentedly. Yet, the reality is the opposite. People spend their entire lives chasing one form of happiness after another—career success, wealth, loving relationships, exciting experiences, and material possessions—believing the next milestone will finally bring the lasting joy they seek. However, this happiness is often short-lived, and the mind quickly moves on to desire something else.

This constant pursuit illustrates that the happiness we seek in the external world is elusive and temporary; it slips through our fingers the moment we try to grasp it. Paradoxically, the more intensely we run after happiness, the more it seems to escape us, like a mirage in the desert. What we perceive as the solution often marks another beginning of the same cycle of longing.

Moreover, life naturally oscillates between happiness and sorrow. Just as a sine wave rises and falls, our experiences fluctuate between moments of pleasure and phases of pain. No one can experience uninterrupted happiness, nor can anyone completely escape suffering. This dynamic rhythm is the essence of life. In fact, the only time this fluctuation ceases is when life itself does—when the electrocardiogram (ECG) of the heart becomes a flat line, indicating death.

Thus, the search for happiness is not just inevitable; it is the very essence of being alive. However, perhaps we must ask ourselves whether we are looking in the right place. Is lasting happiness found in the ever-changing external world, or is there a deeper, more permanent source within? This enquiry sets the stage for a profound inner journey that humanity has contemplated for centuries.

Money Can Buy Commodities, Not Happiness

There is a common belief that if everyone had abundant wealth and all the comforts of life, they would naturally be happy. On the surface, this seems logical—after all, money can solve many practical problems. It can buy luxurious homes, fancy cars, gourmet food, exotic vacations, and the latest technological gadgets. However, a deeper examination of the lives of the super-rich and the financially successful reveals that they are not necessarily happier than those with fewer material possessions. In fact, they often face unique challenges that money simply cannot resolve.

Having enough money eliminates certain struggles, particularly the hardship of meeting basic needs like food, shelter, clothing, and healthcare. However, life's challenges do not end there. While money can address issues related to poverty, it does not safeguard anyone from the more subtle yet equally painful forms of suffering. There are countless things that money cannot buy, regardless of how much one possesses. **For instance, peace of mind is not a purchasable commodity.** Wealthy individuals often find themselves under constant pressure to maintain their assets, navigate complex relationships, manage social expectations, and confront the fear of losing what they have built. Hence, the burden of wealth can lead to anxiety and sleepless nights.

Similarly, money cannot buy good health. While wealth may provide access to better medical care, no amount of money can guarantee freedom from disease, ageing, or mental distress. Time, another precious asset, is completely beyond the reach of money; no billionaire can purchase even a single extra moment of life when their time comes.

Intangible treasures such as respect, genuine love, integrity, emotional well-being, and meaningful relationships are never available for sale. Respect earned through wealth is often shallow and temporary; true respect comes from one's character, humility, and service to others. Genuine relationships are built on trust, affection, and selflessness—not on how much one spends on gifts or lavish experiences. Emotional health, which forms the foundation of a satisfying life, cannot be acquired through financial transactions.

Regardless of whether one belongs to the wealthy elite, the striving middle class, or the struggling lower class, everyone faces their own set of problems. The rich may face emotional emptiness, trust issues, and social isolation. The middle class battles financial stress, career pressures, and the challenge of maintaining status. The poor struggle for survival and basic dignity. In each scenario, the pursuit of happiness persists, as it remains elusive across all economic layers.

Ultimately, it becomes clear that while money is essential for comfort and convenience, it has its limitations. It can buy material possessions, but not happiness. True happiness is an inner experience, rooted in self-awareness, purpose, gratitude, loving relationships, and spiritual fulfillment. It is something that must be cultivated from within, independent of one's bank balance. The endless pursuit of money in the hope of achieving lasting happiness is a race that never ends, because happiness is not found in the wallet; it is found in the heart.

The Poison of Comparison: The Crow and Peacock Story

Sometimes we think, "If I can just become like this person, I could be happy. I have the same dreams that they have achieved, so if I can reach a certain milestone in life, I will attain happiness." While taking inspiration and learning from others is valuable, we often fall into the trap of unhealthy comparisons.

A crow lived in the forest and was satisfied with life. However, one day, he saw a swan and thought, "This swan is so white, and I am so black. This swan must be the happiest bird in the world." When the crow expressed this to the swan, the latter replied, "Actually, I thought I was the happiest bird around until I saw a parrot that has two colours. I now believe the parrot is the happiest bird in creation."

The crow then approached the parrot, who explained, "I lived a happy life until I saw a peacock. I have only two colours, but the peacock has many." The crow then visited a peacock in the zoo, where he noticed hundreds of people gathered to see it. After the crowd dispersed, the crow approached the peacock. "Dear peacock," the crow said, "you are so beautiful. Every day, thousands come to see you. When people see me, they shoo me away. You must be the happiest bird on the planet." **The peacock replied, "I always thought that I was the most beautiful and happiest bird. However, because of my beauty, I am entrapped in this zoo**. After examining the zoo, I have realized that the crow is the only bird free from a cage. For the past few days, I have been thinking that if I were a crow, I could happily roam everywhere."

What is Real Happiness and Fulfillment?

When we eat something enjoyable, we experience happiness and contentment, at least temporarily, as our hunger and desire for taste are satisfied. This is similar for our other senses, including hearing, smelling, touching, and seeing, which seek their own means of gratification. The Bhagavad Gita states that all living beings possess both gross and subtle senses. As sentient beings, we are souls covered by gross senses like our eyes, ears, tongue, nose, and skin, as well as by subtle senses, including our mind, intelligence, and false ego. The gross senses are satisfied by tangible objects, while the subtle senses find satisfaction in activities such as solving puzzles, playing mind games, and engaging in intellectual challenges. However, as we discussed earlier, we are neither the gross body nor the subtle body. We are spirit souls encased in these bodies. Therefore, the happiness derived from these senses is not our true happiness.

Real happiness, as stated in the Vedic scriptures, is the happiness of the soul, i.e. spiritual happiness. This spiritual happiness is not merely a state of mind, as is often claimed, but rather a state of the spirit soul. The Vedas describe the inherent characteristics of the soul, which animates this otherwise lifeless body: *Sat* (eternal existence), *Cit* (full of knowledge), and *Ananda* (full of bliss). Happiness, therefore, is not something to be achieved externally; it requires a shift in consciousness from outside to within. **As is sometimes said, the only way OUT is to go WITHIN.** An apt example is the musk deer, which searches for the very fragrance emanating from its own body.

We tend to identify ourselves with our body. For instance, two individuals may be sitting in a car, but one identifies himself as the owner. When anything happens to the car, he feels pain because he thinks, "This is my car." Conversely, the other person, who does not view the car as his own, remains unaffected when a dent occurs simply because he thinks, "It's not my car anyway." Each of us perceives our body as "mine", and thus when anything happens to our gross or subtle bodies, we mistakenly believe it's happening to us.

As mentioned earlier, there is a Vedic injunction: *Asango ayam purushah*, meaning the spirit soul has no connection with the changes of the material body. The body undergoes six changes: birth, growth, sustenance, by-products, dwindling, and ultimately, annihilation. However, the soul undergoes no such alterations. **The soul is always pure and uncontaminated by material attachment.** It remains separate from the body and always retains its intrinsic characteristics of *Sat, Cit*, and *Ananda.* The soul, by nature, is happy and constantly strives to return to its original state of bliss. Therefore, true happiness, which is our very constitutional nature, can be obtained only when we break our identification with the gross and subtle bodies and realize ourselves as spirit souls. There is no other way to achieve genuine happiness.

The Material World - A Temporary Place of Misery

Further, in the Bhagavad Gita, Verse 8.15, Lord Krishna describes the material world we inhabit with two adjectives: temporary and miserable. He explains that everything created will last only for a short while before being annihilated. In fact, everything in this world decays over time, a reality we all experience in our daily lives. Each of us desires unlimited happiness for an unlimited duration, but what we typically encounter is fleeting happiness mixed with significant misery. **Even those who are wealthy and powerful often find themselves *comfortably* miserable.**

The Vedas identify three types of miseries: those caused by the body and mind, those caused by other living beings, and those caused by natural calamities. We may believe, "That won't happen to me," but more often than not, we face a hard reality. In this world, the stark truth is that we do not always receive what we desire and sometimes get what we do not want, both situations leading to sorrow.

There can be a significant contrast between our public persona on social media and our private reality. A relevant story illustrates this point. A man scheduled an appointment with a psychologist. He said to him, "Doctor, no matter what I do, I feel depressed. I just don't know what to do." The psychologist replied, "Come with me to the window." The man followed him. The psychologist pointed outside and said, "Do you see that tent in the distance? A circus is in town, and it is fantastic! There are many acts, especially those of clowns. There is one clown in particular who is extremely funny. If you go see that clown, I guarantee you will not feel depressed again!" With sad eyes, the man responded, **"Doctor, I am that clown!"**

CHAPTER 5

GOD - IS THERE REALLY SOMEONE UP THERE?

Why Happy Birthdays?

We earlier discussed that understanding the soul is a valuable investment, perhaps the best one. There are two significant days in our lives: the day we receive our human body, and the day we discover the purpose of that body. That's why, spiritually speaking, our birthdays are truly "Happy Birthdays". These are the days when, after passing through 8 million other carriers, the soul finally receives a human form.

Additionally, knowing about God represents one of the best uses of our time and energy. But why is this the case? One primary reason, as stated in the Bhagavad Gita, is that the soul is a part and parcel of God.

Hence, knowing about God is crucial to the process of knowing oneself. However, the first step is to believe in the existence of God as a supremely powerful, sentient being who is omniscient, omnipresent, and the Supreme Controller of all that exists.

The Atheistic Conclusion - I Didn't See Anyone Up There

A Russian leader once remarked, "Our astronaut flew into space but didn't see any God there." Such comments often lead people to question whether there is indeed a higher power. There are those who pray to God, but feel they receive no response to their prayers. As a result, they conclude that God doesn't exist. A common argument against God's existence is the problem of suffering in this world: If a just and kind God exists, why is there suffering? Shouldn't the world be free of pain if there is indeed a Supreme Controller? Shouldn't it resemble Paradise if there is a God who is both All-Good and All-Powerful?

Furthermore, some self-proclaimed spiritual leaders assert that God is merely the greatest lie ever invented by those who feel helpless. Mainstream science has also fostered an atheistic notion in our society by disregarding God. While Dolly, the first cloned sheep, garnered significant attention, the original sheep's creation receives no recognition. The inventor of the camera received accolades, whereas the eye—the original camera—allegedly evolved by chance. Artificial satellites in space are meticulously designed and controlled by scientific teams, but planets, according to some, are floating in space by chance. They suggest that our universe evolved from an explosion, the Big Bang, and no Superior energy had a role in its creation. If humanity evolved from monkeys, why do monkeys still exist? These assertions seem far-fetched and fail to satisfy the curiosity of humankind.

Logical Proofs for the Existence of God

Consider a beautiful plastic flower which requires a small factory to be created. Even though it may look attractive, exhibit perfect symmetry, and showcase vibrant colours, it is ultimately lifeless. Now, consider a real flower. It not only displays superior symmetry, colour, and structure, but also possesses additional features such as fragrance, softness, reproductive capability, and sometimes even taste. It is a complex living organism that grows, decays, and perpetuates its species. Yet, many materialistic thinkers argue that this original, living flower arose out of nature by chance, without any deliberate intelligence behind it. Nature, they claim, automatically produces all that we behold—the trees, rivers, mountains, birds, animals, and even the complex human body. Nature is said to be the ultimate cause behind every effect. In this perspective, nature is elevated to the status of a creator, an all-encompassing force that generates, maintains, and eventually destroys.

However, this notion of Nature being an independent creator is incomplete and logically flawed. Every machine, whether simple or complex, necessarily presupposes a maker. A machine is defined as a system of interrelated parts working together to perform specific functions. No machine comes into existence without purposeful design and intelligent intervention. Even a basic mechanical device, such as a wristwatch, necessitates intricate design, assembly, and guiding intelligence. If something as simple as a watch or a plastic flower needs intelligence for its creation, how much more intelligence is needed for the highly complex, self-sustaining, and purpose-driven systems found in nature?

Furthermore, machines lack intentionality. They cannot plan, feel, desire, or adapt beyond their programmed capabilities. They cannot initiate actions on their own. A machine is merely a tool that executes the purpose given to it by its creator. In contrast, living beings exhibit intentionality, desires, and purposefulness. They strive for survival, seek happiness, reproduce, and adapt—

often in ways far more sophisticated than any man-made machine. While the Bhagavad Gita and other Vedic scriptures acknowledge that Nature produces countless things automatically, they also affirm that Nature is not independent; it is created and governed by a supreme intelligent being, i.e. God.

Nature can be likened to a sophisticated, automated factory, but even such a factory requires a designer, a programmer, an operator, and a source of raw materials. Left to itself, the factory cannot function. The automated processes of nature are simply manifestations of the underlying divine intelligence that orchestrates the material world with precision and purpose.

Addressing the Problem of Suffering

When confronted with the existence of suffering in this world, some people argue against the benevolence or even the existence of God. However, a practical and common-sense analogy helps us understand this issue. God can be compared to an independent and impartial judge. The judge does not arbitrarily punish or reward; rather, he simply applies the laws that are in place. When a person commits a crime, the punishment is administered according to the law, not because the judge personally desires to cause harm. Similarly, the rewards and punishments experienced by living beings in this world are the result of their own past actions, governed by the laws of karma. God does not cruelly inflict suffering; rather, He has established a perfectly just system that imparts consequences for every action, ensuring balance and fairness.

Just as a nation has laws to maintain order, the universe is governed by moral and natural laws established by God. Those who live in accordance with these divine laws experience harmony and happiness, while those who violate them face correction, not as a sign of divine vengeance, but as a means of reformation and learning.

The Burden of Proof

Another flawed argument often presented by atheists is the categorical denial of God's existence. Logically, to say definitively that "God does not exist" requires one to possess absolute, all-encompassing knowledge of everything that exists in the universe and beyond. To claim that there is no gold in China, one must have thoroughly searched every inch of the country. Similarly, to assert that God does not exist would require the claimant to have complete knowledge of all dimensions, times, and places, which no human possesses. Such a claim is, therefore, inherently presumptuous and intellectually dishonest.

Although most of us have not seen God directly, His existence is evident through the vast amount of circumstantial and inferential evidence observable in the world around us. The unseen can often be understood through the seen. For example, when we see a house, we infer the existence of a builder, even if we never meet him. Likewise, when we see a painting, we know there is an artist behind it. In the same way, the beautiful and meticulously organized universe points to the existence of a supreme designer.

In the Bhagavad Gita, Verse 7.7, Lord Krishna provides an instructive analogy: just as pearls in a necklace are strung together by a thread that is not immediately visible, all beings and objects in this world are connected and held together by the unseen power of God. The remarkable order and regularity in nature—the rising and setting of the sun, the precise orbit of planets, the changing of seasons, and the perfect distance of earth from the sun, all indicate the presence of a regulator and sustainer. This precision is not random; it is intentional.

Modern science has indeed discovered that such order exists at microscopic and even subatomic levels. The double-helix structure of DNA, the molecular interactions within a living cell, and the precise constants in physics that govern the universe, all testify to an extraordinary degree of order and fine-tuning. Yet, despite uncovering these intricacies, scientists have not been able to create life from non-living matter. The smallest living cell, invisible to the naked eye, contains incredibly complex systems—mechanisms for food production, energy transport, waste disposal, and reproduction. Who designed this astonishing level of organization?

Additionally, nature operates under a web of mathematical, physical, chemical, and biological laws. Laws do not write themselves; they are indicators of intelligence and governance. When we observe laws in human society, we naturally conclude there is a lawmaker behind them. Similarly, the laws of nature point to a cosmic lawmaker—God.

There is an English saying: "For the spiritualist, God is the beginning; for the scientist, God is the end." In other words, while spirituality begins with the assumption of God's existence, science—when pursued with open and honest enquiry—often leads to the inescapable conclusion that an intelligent cause underlies the observable universe.

Big Bang or Big Brain?

This leads us to the crucial question: Did everything begin with a Big Bang or a Big Brain? According to the Big Bang theory, everything emerged from a point of infinite temperature, infinite density, and infinitesimal size—a state that is physically indescribable and mathematically unverifiable. But where did this initial singularity come from? What caused it? If time and space themselves began with the Big Bang, then what existed before it? How can something come from nothing?

Atheism often posits that there was nothing, and then nothing exploded for no reason, leading to the creation of everything. Subsequently, a portion of this everything somehow rearranged itself, purely by chance, into complex self-replicating molecules, which eventually resulted in dinosaurs, and later, human beings capable of writing books and composing music. This chain of events, presented without any guiding intelligence, is not only improbable but defies common sense.

Imagine a scenario where an explosion occurs in a printing press, and somehow, the debris magically arranges itself into a perfectly bound dictionary. Would any rational person accept such an explanation? The probability of the universe, with all its fine-tuned constants and life-supporting parameters, assembling itself by random chance is exponentially lower than that of a printing press explosion producing a dictionary. Yet, this is the explanation proposed by atheism.

In contrast, the Vedic scriptures offer a more reasonable and satisfying answer: the universe did not emerge from a random explosion but from the purposeful design of the Supreme Intelligence—God. The Bhagavatam describes how creation unfolds not from a chaotic blast, but from the deliberate glance and will of the Lord upon material nature, initiating a carefully ordered process.

When we examine the world around us with an open mind and heart, the existence of God becomes not only believable, but evident. The beauty, complexity, order, morality, and purpose that pervade the universe are not accidental; they reflect the fingerprints of the divine.

In summary, the argument that Nature is an independent creator is logically insufficient. Nature is akin to a sophisticated machine—it functions automatically, but it is neither self-originating nor self-sustaining without an intelligent operator. God is that supreme creator and operator. He is the ultimate cause of all causes, the invisible designer who orchestrates both the seen and unseen aspects of existence.

Rather than blindly accepting the improbability of chance-driven creation, it is more reasonable, more aligned with experience, and more in harmony with common sense to acknowledge the presence of an intelligent, conscious designer—God. Far from being a blind leap of faith, belief in God is a logical conclusion supported by both observation and deep philosophical enquiry.

Yes, Do Not Accept Blindly, But Do Not Reject Blindly Either

As with any field of knowledge, this domain is also filled with misconceptions and varying perspectives, including those of agnostics, skeptics, believers, followers, and atheists. As we discussed earlier, we should not believe anything blindly. However, if authentic information is received from credible sources in this field and is supported by our own observations, experiences, and logic, we must also avoid blindly rejecting the same. **One must neither be a sentimental atheist nor a blind believer; conclusions should be based on reason and logic**. On this neutral rational premise, let's move ahead to understand the topic.

The greatest proof of a superior power in existence is creation—the existence of this material world. Intelligent design, as stated by Michael Behe, an American biochemist staunchly advocating the concept of "irreducible complexity of essential cellular structures", illustrates this point. As a layperson, one can infer from his claims that there is incredible design in creation, down to the smallest unit of life. A professor and author of the 1996 bestseller, *Darwin's Black Box*, Behe challenges the classical neo-Darwinian explanation that intricate cell structures arose by chance. He uses the example of a bacterial flagellum to introduce the concept of "irreducible complexity". If a structure is so complex that all its parts must initially be present in a suitably functioning manner, it is said to be irreducibly complex. All the parts of a bacterial flagellum must be present from the start to function at all. According to Darwinian theory, any component that doesn't offer an advantage to an organism (i.e., doesn't function) would be lost or discarded. The question of how such a structure could have evolved in a gradual, step-by-step process, as required by classical Darwinian evolution, presents a significant challenge to evolutionists. Furthermore, the way a flagellum is used adds an additional layer of complexity to the discussion.

Thus, we conclude that order exists both on a micro level and a macro level. From the minutest cell to the gargantuan galaxies, one cannot deny the design or the existence of a sentient designer. It simply does not make sense. Hence, it is difficult to genuinely be an atheist. We are surrounded by evidence. Practically everything in the world, including our own bodies—which contain multiple systems such as the digestive, nervous, and respiratory systems—strongly implies the existence of a superintelligent being. Common sense, logical reasoning, and even scientific understanding strongly indicate that there must be a supremely intelligent being—the creator and maintainer of this intricately-designed world.

Can I See God?

One of the most common arguments against the existence of God is rooted in empiricism—the belief that "seeing is believing". According to this view, only that which can be directly perceived by our five senses should be accepted as truth. Since God cannot be seen, some people prematurely conclude that He does not exist. However, this argument is quite weak and superficial because even within this material world, there are countless objects and forces that are not directly observable, yet no one doubts their existence.

For example, we cannot see electrons, but we know they exist due to their observable effects in electricity and chemical reactions. Similarly, we cannot see mobile networks or radio waves, but we experience their presence every day through our phones, televisions, and radios. We cannot see gravitational force or magnetic fields, yet their influence is undeniable. Even the five elements mentioned in the Bhagavad Gita—earth, water, fire, air, and ether (space)—illustrate a gradation from the gross to the subtle. For example, space is subtler than air, and the mind is even subtler than space. No one has seen the mind or touched it, yet we are fully convinced of its existence through our experiences of thoughts, desires, and emotions.

Beyond the mind lies the soul, which is even subtler, and beyond the soul is God, who is the subtlest of all. If something as fundamental as the mind cannot be perceived through our gross senses, then how can we expect to perceive God, who is described as the transcendental reality beyond even the soul? Therefore, the limitation lies not in God's visibility, but in our current capacity to perceive Him.

To perceive anything in this world, one must possess the appropriate tools and methods. For instance, if someone wants to see the butter hidden in milk, they must first turn the milk into yogurt and then churn it properly. Similarly, to see a distant star, one must use a telescope; to see microorganisms, a microscope is necessary. If someone wishes to see Antarctica, they must undertake the necessary travel arrangements—obtaining a passport, visa, and tickets—and then physically go there. One cannot sit at home and deny the existence of Antarctica simply because they have never seen it.

In the same way, there is a process to perceive God. This process is known as yoga, especially the path of Bhakti Yoga, which is the yoga of devotion. God can indeed be seen—but not with dull or untrained senses. The spiritual senses must be purified and awakened through the practice of devotion, meditation, study of sacred texts, association with saintly persons, and cultivation of qualities like humility, patience, and faith. It is illogical to demand to see God without first following the necessary spiritual discipline. This is akin to a blind person insisting on seeing the sun while refusing to undergo treatment to restore their vision. The sun certainly exists, but until the blind person regains their sight, they cannot perceive it.

Similarly, until we purify our senses and heart, we remain blind to the presence of God, who is all around us and within us. It is not that God is absent; it is that we are not yet qualified to see Him. The good news is that Vedic scriptures and great spiritual teachers consistently assure us that by sincerely following the prescribed process, we can eventually see God face to face. There is indeed someone "up there" and all around us. Let us embark on the path to discover who that is.

CHAPTER 6

GOD - A SUPREME POWER OR A SUPREMELY POWERFUL PERSON?

The Irony of Atheism

In the previous chapter, we established the reality of God: He is NOT the greatest lie created by those who feel helpless and depend upon a superior power for support. He is NOT simply a principle or a concept—He is the absolute Truth, and He exists as surely as we do. We are surrounded by evidence of this Truth. Thus, it is far easier to be a theist than to be an atheist.

One of my favourite quotes about atheism is given below:

Atheism. The belief that there was nothing and nothing happened to nothing and then nothing magically exploded for no reason, creating everything, and then a bunch of everything magically rearranged itself for no reason whatsoever into self-replicating bits which then turned into dinosaurs. Makes perfect sense.

It's hilarious, isn't it? So, yes, it's much easier to be a theist and discover proofs of God's existence every moment of every day, focusing on the multitude of miracles around us that we often mistake for ordinary occurrences.

Now we come to a critical question: If God does exist, is He a Principle, a Supreme Power, an infinite blinding light, or is He a person—more specifically, *the* Supreme Person? Let's delve deeper into this topic.

Gross and Subtle Things in Existence

There are various levels of existence: gross, subtle, subtler, and subtlest. Entities like electrons, protons, subatomic particles, bacteria, and viruses are examples of subtle forms of existence, as they are not visible to the naked eye, yet undeniably exist. Even matter itself transitions from gross to subtle. For example, air is subtler than solid objects, and space is even subtler than air. We cannot see, touch, smell, hear, or taste space, yet we accept its existence, and science supports this acceptance.

Subtler than space are the mind and intelligence. We all acknowledge that everyone has a mind distinct from the brain, which is gross matter. Our minds and intelligence enable us to think and make distinctions, respectively, but no one can directly perceive their own or any other person's mind and intelligence.

God: The Subtlest Entity

According to the Bhagavad Gita, subtler than the mind and intelligence is the living being, or the soul, which is the essence of our true selves. The soul is an extremely tiny spiritual spark, invisible to both the naked eye and the finest microscopes. Nevertheless, it exists and animates the body. When the soul leaves the body, we refer to it as death; when it enters a new body, we call it birth. Vedic scriptures assert that God exists at a level even subtler than matter and the soul. Therefore, God cannot be perceived through our gross or even subtle senses. This does not imply that God does not exist.

In the Bhagavad Gita, Verse 7.7, a comparison is made to a pearl necklace, which is held together by an invisible string. Although the string is unseen, it is essential for the necklace's existence. Similarly, God is the unseen force that unites everything, though He cannot be observed directly. Just as the Covid virus is detected through symptoms rather than requiring a visual confirmation of the virus itself, the external world is filled with numerous signs that indicate God's existence, even if we cannot see Him with our eyes.

Seeing Through the Ears/ Understanding God Through Listening

Since we cannot directly perceive God, how can we determine whether He is a person, a Principle, a Supreme Power, or an infinite light? Speculating on this matter can lead to erroneous conclusions, which can be dangerous to our lives. Much of our lifestyle is shaped by our mindset, which is influenced by our understanding of ourselves, the world, and God. Hence, relying on trial and error or mere assumptions is not a viable approach.

As discussed in the first chapter of this book, we need certain scientific knowledge that we can depend on. This knowledge must be as certain as mathematics, leaving no room for doubt or revised, corrected, or updated versions. Such understanding is obtained through learning from authoritative sources in any field. In spiritual matters, the authority is the Vedic scriptures. Concepts that cannot be observed directly can be understood through the guidance of these texts, which offer a real vision.

Most of us heard the simple yet profound story of the five blind men and the elephant in our childhood. Each blind man attempts to understand the form of the elephant through touch, smell, sound, etc., leading them to formulate different theories:

one believes the elephant is like a rope, while the others think it resembles a snake, a tree, a fan, and a wall. The truth is revealed by a sixth person, a wise man who comes along and enlightens the five blind men that the elephant is the amalgamation of all their experiences and something even more. The actual form of the elephant is explained by this person to all five blind men, who accept the explanation happily, illustrating a valuable lesson.

In general, we are all "blind" in our understanding of God and whether He has form or is formless. Since God is the subtlest of all entities, understanding Him requires the right qualifications or tools. Therefore, the answer lies in seeing through the ears by hearing from authorized scriptures. Much like we learn from textbooks in school or university, we can accept knowledge about the form of God from the authorized textbooks—the Vedas, Bhagavad Gita, etc.

God is a Person – Vedic Proofs and Logical Reasoning

For example, in the *Aitareya Upanishad* (1.1 & 1.2), there are two profound *sutras: "sa aikshata"*—The Lord glanced over the material creation—and *"sa imal lokan asrijata"*—The Lord created this entire material world. What do they actually signify? The word "glanced" inherently implies that the Lord possesses eyes. Eyes naturally indicate the presence of a face, and a face suggests that He has a form. However, this form is not mundane like ours; it is described as a transcendental, spiritual form because this event took place before the creation of the material elements. Since this predates the manifestation of the material world, the Lord's eyes are not made of earth, water, fire, air, or ether like our physical bodies are. This emphasizes that the Supreme Lord has a personal form that is beyond the limitations of the material creation.

There are numerous other scriptural references supporting the idea that God has a form. For example, when we offer prayers, it is often stated that the Lord hears them. Hearing presupposes that He has ears. In the Bhagavad Gita (9.22), Krishna states that He reciprocates with His devotees. How can someone reciprocate if they lack personality or form? Similarly, in the *Brahma Samhita* (5.1), it is stated: "*ishvarah paramah krishnah sac-cid-ananda-vigrahah*" Krishna is the Supreme Lord; He possesses a form (*vigraha*) that is eternal (*sat*), full of knowledge (*cit*), and full of bliss (*ananda*). The use of the word "*vigraha*" is extremely significant; it refers to a form, but not a temporary or decaying one like those of material bodies. His form is transcendental, immutable, and beyond the dualities of matter.

When we contemplate the concept of attraction, it becomes even more logical that God must have form. Beauty inherently resides in form; the eyes are naturally drawn to forms, shapes, colours, and symmetry. We seldom hear of anyone becoming captivated by something completely abstract or impersonal. Even when people speak of concepts like "energy" or "light", they try to visualize them in tangible terms. Human consciousness naturally seeks relationships, faces, and personalities. It is the personal element that deeply satisfies the heart.

God is described as Krishna, which literally means "the all-attractive one". How can someone be all-attractive yet formless? This is contradictory. Attraction requires qualities, beauty, charm, and reciprocation—all features of a person. In the Bhagavad Gita (7.7), Krishna declares, "There is no truth superior to Me." If God is the ultimate reality, He cannot lack personality because personality is the most evolved state of existence. If impersonal energy were the ultimate, then personality—being a higher expression—would not logically originate from something lower.

Therefore, it is consistent to conclude that the Absolute Truth is ultimately a person.

Additionally, the Bible states that man is made in the image of God. If man has form, feelings, senses, and the ability to relate, it is only logical that these qualities reflect the nature of the Supreme Being, from whom everything emanates. The Vedas also declare, "*janmady asya yatah*"—the Absolute Truth is that from which everything comes. If forms, senses, and personalities exist in this world, they must ultimately originate from the Supreme, who is the original source.

If everything in creation has form, how can the original creator be entirely formless? This doesn't make sense. The effect cannot possess qualities absent in the cause. A potter can make pots because he has the capacity, intelligence, and form to do so. Similarly, the creator of the universe must inherently possess the attributes evident within creation, but in their perfect, unlimited form.

Thus, the Vedic conclusion is clear: God is a transcendental person, full of beauty, qualities, and infinite attractiveness—not limited by material constraints, but possessing an eternal, blissful form that is the source of all.

God is Impersonal - Proofs in the Vedas

However, in the same scriptures that refer to God's beautiful form, there are verses indicating that God is *arupa* and *nirakara*, which means without form, and *nirguna*, meaning without any material qualities, changeless and inactive. This refers to the impersonal *Brahman* or the dazzling, unlimited glowing light known as the *Brahmajyoti*. The *Brahman*, the Absolute Truth, is referred to as the Greatest, Unlimited, Indescribable, Inconceivable, Attributeless, Beyond Thought, and Beyond Language. The Vedic injunction "*tamaso ma jyotir gamaya*" exhorts one to move from darkness unto light. Which light is being referenced here? It is the *Brahmajyoti*, the infinite effulgence pervading the spiritual sky and existing everywhere, beyond all limitations.

The scriptures describe that all light within this material world—including the brilliance of the sun, the cooling rays of the moon, and the countless sparkling stars—ultimately originates from this *Brahmajyoti*. It is said in the Bhagavad Gita (15.6) that the spiritual world is self-illuminating and does not require the light of the sun or moon because it is fully pervaded by this spiritual effulgence. The *Brahmajyoti* exists beyond the material universe, and it forms the boundary between the spiritual and material realms.

When the Vedas speak of God as formless and without attributes, they refer to this all-pervasive, impersonal aspect of the Supreme. The Upanishads often highlight this feature to help the soul transcend material attachments and realize that the Absolute Truth is beyond the limited forms and qualities of the material world. Meditating on the *Brahman* can liberate the soul from the bondage of matter and lead to the experience of spiritual light and peace. This realization, however, is considered incomplete without understanding the personal aspect of God. Nonetheless, the impersonal *Brahman* is a valid and important revelation in the Vedic tradition, representing the infinite, all-pervading energy of the Supreme.

A Perfect Reconciliation – God is Both Personal and Impersonal at the Same Time

One of the most profound insights presented in the Vedic scriptures is the perfect reconciliation of what often seems like an irresolvable contradiction—that God is simultaneously personal and impersonal. Many philosophical debates, both ancient and modern, have tried to establish either of these aspects as the sole definition of the Supreme. Some conclude that God is impersonal, an all-pervading spiritual energy without form or attributes. Others argue that God must ultimately be a person, endowed with form, qualities, and transcendental pastimes. But is it necessary to view them as mutually exclusive? The answer, revealed in the deepest layers of Vedic wisdom, is that both these seemingly opposite descriptions are simultaneously true.

The *Ishopanishad*, revered as the chief among the 108 principal Upanishads, beautifully harmonizes these two perspectives. In Mantra 5, it states: "The Supreme Lord walks and does not walk. He is far away, but He is very near as well. He is within everything, and yet He is outside of everything." At first glance, this appears paradoxical. How can someone both walk and not walk at the same time? How can someone be distant and near simultaneously? This mantra points to the Supreme Lord's inconceivable nature—He exists beyond the limitations of mundane logic. It is not that one aspect negates the other; rather, He encompasses all contradictions in perfect harmony. His impersonal energy pervades everything, yet He personally resides in His eternal, transcendental abode.

The *Srimad Bhagavatam* (1.2.11) provides further clarity by stating: "Learned transcendentalists who know the Absolute Truth call this non-dual substance Brahman, Paramatma, or Bhagavan." This profound verse reveals that the Absolute Truth is realized in three phases: *Brahman* (the impersonal, all-pervading spiritual effulgence), *Paramatma* (the localized Supersoul present within the heart of every living being and within every atom), and *Bhagavan* (the Supreme Person possessing all transcendental opulences in their entirety). These are not three separate entities but rather three progressive realizations of the same Absolute Truth. This can be compared to seeing the sun in different ways: as sunlight scattered across the sky, as the sun's surface seen from a distance, and as the blazing sun globe itself.

The impersonal *Brahman* is the glowing spiritual effulgence that emanates from the transcendental body of the Supreme Lord. The *Paramatma* is His localized expansion within all beings, guiding them as the ultimate overseer and witness. *Bhagavan* is the Supreme Personality of Godhead, the original source of both *Brahman* and *Paramatma*. Therefore, a complete understanding of the Supreme requires the acceptance of all three aspects. Just as different limbs and features together form a complete body, *Brahman, Paramatma*, and *Bhagavan* together reveal the full picture of the Absolute Truth. To emphasize this point, the analogy of the elephant and the blind men is often given. Each blind man touches a different part of the elephant and concludes, based on limited perception, that the elephant is like a rope, a wall, a pipe, and so on. However, the elephant encompasses all of these features and more. Only when one steps back and perceives the elephant in totality does one arrive at the complete truth.

Which among these three features—*Brahman, Paramatma*, or *Bhagavan*—is the original? This question is answered in the Bhagavad Gita (14.27), where Lord Krishna declares: "I am the basis of the impersonal Brahman, which is the constitutional position of ultimate happiness, and which is immortal, imperishable, and eternal." Krishna clearly states that the *Brahman* effulgence emanates from Him. The impersonal light is not independent; it relies upon His supreme, personal form. Just as sunlight cannot exist without the sun, *Brahman* cannot exist without its source—the Supreme Personality of Godhead.

Let us further understand this concept through a simple yet powerful analogy. Imagine someone standing at a seashore for the first time, at night, having never seen a ship before. In the distance, he sees a glowing light. Excited, he runs back to his village, proclaiming, "I have seen a ship! A ship is nothing but light!" Technically, he is not wrong; he did see the light. However, is his understanding complete? No. Had he waited until daylight, he would have realized that the ship is not just the light; it has a vast structure, decks, passengers, engines, and much more. The light is an inseparable part of the ship, but not the entirety of it. Similarly, the impersonal *Brahman* is but a partial realization of the Supreme Lord. The *Brahman* emanates from Him just as light radiates from the sun.

The *Ishopanishad* further corroborates this in Mantra 15, where the devotee offers a heartfelt prayer: "O my Lord, O primeval philosopher, maintainer of the universe, O regulator of the living entities, please remove the effulgence of Your transcendental rays so that I can see Your form of bliss." The sincere seeker does not wish to remain satisfied with the dazzling *Brahman* realization; he desires to behold the beautiful, personal form of the Lord hidden behind that effulgence.

Thus, the complete resolution of the personal versus impersonal debate is that the Supreme Lord eternally possesses both features, but His personal aspect is primary. The personal form of *Bhagavan* is the superset, while *Brahman* and *Paramatma* are subsets. The ultimate goal is to realize *Bhagavan*, the Supreme Person, the source of all beauty, knowledge, wealth, strength, fame, and renunciation. In Sanskrit, the word "*Bhagavan*" precisely describes the one who possesses these six opulences in full. Just as the word "*Vidvan*" refers to a learned person and

"*Dhanavan*" to a wealthy person, "*Bhagavan*" refers to the one who is supremely opulent in all respects.

The most perfect expression of *Bhagavan* is Krishna, whose very name means "the all-attractive one". He attracts all living beings through His limitless qualities and transcendental pastimes. In this way, the Supreme Lord is not confined to any one-sided concept. He is simultaneously the impersonal *Brahman*, the omnipresent *Paramatma*, and the supremely charming *Bhagavan*. Understanding this harmony provides the key to unlocking the complete knowledge of the Absolute Truth.

Q.E.D. – *Quod Erat Demonstrandum*. The divine riddle is solved.

CHAPTER 7

AM I GOD, AND IS EVERYONE GOD, TOO?

Why is this Important to Understand?

Let's now discuss the most crucial aspect of spirituality in one's spiritual life. Why is it the most important? This is so because a slight misunderstanding can lead to disastrous results in one's spiritual life. Just as even a one-degree deviation from the intended flight path can cause an airplane to land thousands of miles off course, so too can a small error in spiritual understanding lead one astray. Consider how someone might shave smoothly with a sharp razor, only to nick themselves due to a moment of inattention. There is a Vedic injunction that states: *"Ksurasya dhara nisita duratyaya, durgam pathas tat kavayo vadanti"*. This means that the path of spirituality is fraught with obstacles and is akin to walking on a razor's edge. One needs to be clear of all types of misunderstandings. Ignorance is not an excuse. Just as a driver must know the rules of the road, a spiritual seeker must understand the necessary principles of spiritual practice. Therefore, it is essential to approach a spiritual master or Guru—someone who accurately knows the path to spiritual success.

While there are many concepts to clarify on the path of spirituality, one major topic is whether there is one God or if everyone is God, as some spiritualists claim. There are many shades to this. Sometimes, the followers of a particular Guru declare their Guru to be God, while some spiritual masters proclaim themselves as God. Others assert that every single person, nay, every single living being, is God. Additionally, some say that Hinduism is a broad religion with multiple Gods from which individuals can choose, like selecting dishes from a buffet. Unfortunately, this has led to significant confusion in this vital area of spirituality. Innocent seekers may be misled if they are not careful. Let's address the confusion and uncover clarity.

Definition of God in the Vedas

When we acquire a new electronic device, like a television set or a washing machine, it typically comes with a manual provided by the manufacturer. This manual contains authentic information about the product, and no one can offer better insights than the company that created it. This manual would also include information about the company or firm that has developed the product. Similarly, when the world was created, God—who is the manufacturer of this world—provided a manual. As previously discussed, the order and design found in this world indicate the existence of an Intelligent Designer, who is God. Along with authentic information about this world, there is information about its manufacturer, God. The timeless Vedas and the Bhagavad Gita serve as the manuals containing essential information about the world, God, and our lives. No one can provide more credible knowledge on these concepts than the Vedas. Therefore, we must seek understanding of who God is only from the Vedas, the Bhagavad Gita, and authentic Gurus who adhere to their teachings.

The Vedas and the Bhagavad Gita, along with supplementary literature, provide information on whether there is one God or many, whether a Guru can be God, and whether each individual can claim to be God. Let us discuss these issues one by one, starting with ourselves: Are we God? The definition of God, or the Sanskrit word "*Bhagavan*", which is a popular word at least in India, is given in the *Parasara Samhita,* written by Parasara Muni, the father of Vyasadeva. He states that the Supreme Personality who possesses all riches, all strength, all fame, all beauty, all knowledge, and all renunciation is called *Bhagavan*. While many people exhibit wealth, power, beauty, fame, intelligence, and detachment, no one can claim to possess all these qualities entirely. God is characterized as Omnipresent, Omniscient, and Omnipotent. He is the creator, the maintainer of all that exists, and also the destroyer. He is the Supreme Controller and the Proprietor of everything. Only someone who can claim these attributes, along with proof, can be considered God. In the Bhagavad Gita, Lord Krishna affirms His divine status in several verses, including 7.7 and 10.8, where He states that He is the source of everything animate and inanimate, both matter and spirit. He substantiates this claim by revealing His Universal Form to Arjuna. This is recorded in the Mahabharata. Known as an "*Itihasa*", meaning history, the Mahabharata contains within itself the Bhagavad Gita, the song of God. The Universal Form is described in vivid detail in the eleventh chapter of the Bhagavad Gita. This form encompasses the entire sky, featuring thousands of faces, arms, bellies, mouths, and eyes, expanding infinitely with a brilliance comparable to thousands of suns. Arjuna observes that he sees no end, no middle, and no beginning. He also says he recognizes all demigods, including Lord Brahma and Lord Shiva, within this Universal Form.

No one Is or Can Become God

With the definition and qualities of God laid out in the Bhagavad Gita, it becomes clear beyond doubt that no living being is or can ever become God. God, or the Supreme Personality of Godhead, as revealed in the Gita, possesses exclusive and unparalleled attributes: He is omnipresent, omniscient, omnipotent, the ultimate source of all that exists, the Supreme Proprietor of everything, the Absolute Controller of all worlds, and the Maintainer and Sustainer of both the animate and inanimate creation. These divine characteristics are eternally intrinsic to God alone. None of us can claim to possess these qualities at any point in time. Even the most elevated living beings, demigods or liberated souls, cannot exhibit these unlimited features.

Certain spiritual paths, particularly those influenced by impersonalist or monistic philosophies, claim that the individual soul is ultimately God and that upon attaining liberation, one merges with the Supreme and becomes God. However, the Bhagavad Gita strongly refutes this notion. In Verse 15.7, Lord Krishna declares: "*mamaivamsho jiva-loke jiva-bhutah sanatanah*"—The living entities in this conditioned world are My eternal, fragmental parts. The word "*sanatanah*" (eternal) is significant here. It emphasizes that our constitutional position as subordinate parts of the Supreme Lord is everlasting. We are eternally dependent on God, and this relationship of servitude and connection never changes, even in the liberated state.

The belief that a soul can become God is not only philosophically incorrect but also dangerous, as it opens the door for impostors to deceive people by falsely claiming divinity. Genuine spiritual realization involves understanding that we are eternally servants of God, not competitors with Him. True liberation is about reviving our loving relationship with the Supreme, not usurping His position.

Everyone or Everything Cannot Be God

It is a fundamental misunderstanding to believe that everyone or everything is God. Since a single soul is neither God nor can it become God, it logically follows that not everyone can be God either. In fact, the concept that everyone is God, or that everything in the universe is God—commonly known as pantheism—is flawed. If we assert that everyone is God, then the uniqueness, supremacy, and significance of God are immediately lost. God is defined as the Supreme Being, the Ultimate Controller, the Creator, the Maintainer, and the One who is omnipotent, omniscient, and omnipresent. If everyone were God, there would be no hierarchy, no ultimate authority, and no supreme controller. The idea is as illogical as saying that everyone in a company can simultaneously be the CEO. By definition, a CEO is a unique individual who holds the highest position in the organization, directing and overseeing its overall operations. Others in the company may hold important roles and have significant responsibilities, but they are subordinate to the CEO and cannot all claim that singular post.

Similarly, some spiritual organizations propose that we are actually God but have simply forgotten our divine status due to illusion or ignorance. According to them, once we remember who we truly are, we regain our identity as God. However, this argument is fundamentally flawed. God, by definition, is the Supreme Being, never subject to illusion, forgetfulness, or ignorance. If God can fall into illusion and forget His own divinity, it logically implies that illusion is more powerful than God. Such a conclusion directly contradicts the essential characteristics of God as described in the Vedic scriptures.

What about scriptural statements like "*Aham Brahmasmi*" (I am *Brahman*), "*Soham*" (I am He), and "*Tat Tvam Asi*" (You are that)? These statements are sometimes misinterpreted to suggest that the individual soul is identical in all respects to God. However, Vedic literature presents both types of statements—some indicating the similarity between God and the soul, and others emphasizing the difference. The key is to properly reconcile these two perspectives.

The *Katha Upanishad* (2.2.13) offers a perfect reconciliation: "*nityo nityanam chetanas cetananam eko bahunam yo vidadhati kaman*"—Among all the eternal entities, there is One Supreme Eternal. Among all conscious beings, there is One Supreme Conscious Being who is maintaining and fulfilling the desires of everyone else. This verse clearly distinguishes the Supreme Lord from the countless living entities. The living entities are eternal and conscious, but the Lord is the chief among them.

The proper conclusion, therefore, is that the soul is a minute spark of God—qualitatively one with Him, but quantitatively insignificant. Just as a spark from a fire shares the fiery nature of the blaze but is not the whole fire, we are godly in nature but not God. We are eternally subordinate parts of the Supreme Whole. Recognizing this nuanced relationship helps us understand the harmony between oneness and difference as explained in the Vedic scriptures.

The Guru or Spiritual Master is Not God, but a Representative of God

In India, there is an unfortunate trend where self-proclaimed Godmen frequently emerge, often declaring themselves to be God or allowing their followers to glorify them as such. It seems that practically every month, a new "God" appears on the spiritual marketplace. Time and again, the media has exposed several of these so-called Godmen as frauds, yet people continue to fall prey to such deception. Even after repeated warnings and exposures, the cycle persists. Why does this continue? Why are people so easily misled? The answer lies in a combination of human gullibility, emotional vulnerability, and a deep yearning to find someone tangible to worship and follow.

The Vedic scriptures provide clear guidance on this subject. They teach us that the Guru is not God but rather a representative of God. The role of the Guru is supremely important but must be properly understood. A genuine Guru is not someone who claims divinity or demands worship for themselves. Instead, the Guru is a transparent medium who guides the sincere seeker on the path toward God. Just as a pair of spectacles helps a person with impaired vision to see the world clearly, the Guru helps a spiritually blind individual to see the truth of God and understand spiritual reality.

Our current vision is clouded by ignorance, illusion, and material contamination. The Guru, like the spectacles, does not become the object of our vision but rather facilitates our vision. The real Guru is one who has deeply heard and understood the Vedic scriptures from a bona fide source, has practised the principles in their life, and has personally experienced transformative results. Such a Guru is not interested in amassing fame, wealth, or followers. Instead, the true Guru is profoundly devoted to God—immersed in love and service to the Supreme Lord—and, like a humble postman, simply delivers the message of God without any adulteration or personal ambition. They remain faithful to the disciplic succession, a chain that must trace its origin directly to God Himself.

But why do people so often mistake the Guru for God? Why do some Gurus go so far as to declare themselves as God or accept such declarations from their followers? The answer is twofold. First, some of these so-called Gurus are outright charlatans—clever word jugglers who stage dramatic shows to impress people and extract money, power, or adulation. Second, some of these individuals may have acquired mystic powers or yogic perfections (*siddhis*), which can easily allure the uninformed masses.

According to the Vedic scriptures, particularly the descriptions found in Patanjali's *Yoga Sutras* and elaborated in texts like the Srimad Bhagavatam, there are mystic perfections that yogis can attain through the practice of Astanga Yoga. Astanga Yoga involves eight progressive stages: *Yama* (restraints), *Niyama* (regulative principles), *Asana* (physical postures), *Pranayama* (breath control), *Pratyahara* (withdrawal of the senses), *Dharana* (concentration), *Dhyana* (meditation), and *Samadhi* (deep absorption). At the advanced levels of *Dharana*, certain mystic perfections naturally manifest.

There are eight primary mystic *siddhis*:

1. *Anima* – the ability to become smaller than the smallest particle.
2. *Mahima* – the ability to become larger than the largest object.
3. *Laghima* – the ability to become lighter than air.
4. *Prapti* – the power to obtain anything from anywhere.
5. *Isitva* – the power to control nature and material elements.
6. *Vasitva* – the power to control other living beings.
7. *Prakamya* – the ability to fulfill any desire.
8. *Kamavasayitva* – the perfection of achieving whatever one desires at will.

Apart from these, there are secondary mystical abilities as well. Some yogis, upon attaining these powers, abandon their secluded meditation to showcase their abilities to the public—manifesting ashes, producing gold, walking on water, or performing other extraordinary feats. Unfortunately, people often mistake these displays as evidence of divinity.

However, the Vedic conclusion is crystal clear—such *ṣiddhis* do not make a person God. They are merely material powers, extraordinary but still subordinate to the Supreme. In the Bhagavad Gita, Sanjaya refers to Lord Krishna as Yogeshwara, the master of all mystic powers. Unlike yogis who must work diligently to attain these perfections, Krishna possesses them fully and eternally. He is the source of all *siddhis* and effortlessly controls all natural laws. Krishna can manifest entire gold mines, unlimited universes, and the totality of creation. He does not need to practise yoga to acquire powers; He is power personified.

Let us not be misled. A genuine spiritual seeker must carefully examine the credentials of a Guru through the lens of scripture, reason, and the guidance of other qualified devotees. The Guru should never pose as God, but should always point us toward the actual Supreme Lord.

CHAPTER 8

ONE GOD OR MANY GODS

Let's Not Be Deceived by Bogus Self- Proclaimed Godmen

In the last chapter, we agreed not to be misled by so-called Godmen who either proclaim themselves as such or are declared so by their followers. We also recognized that some yogis might acquire certain mystic powers, exhibit abilities that ordinary people cannot perform, and subsequently proclaim themselves as God. However, such yogis are merely glow-worms in comparison to the sun of the Supreme Lord. They have limited power that diminishes with use, while the Supreme Lord, by definition, possesses infinite opulences, including all mystic powers in full. We have also established that no one can become God; God has always been God right from the beginning.

Are the Demigods God?

When we talk about powerful beings in the universe, especially within the Indian spiritual tradition, we encounter a range of personalities who are widely worshipped as "gods" by millions of people. These include Surya (the sun god), Chandra (the moon god), Lord Ganesha (the remover of obstacles), Lord Indra (the god of rain and king of heaven), Mother Durga (the divine protector), Mother Kali (the fierce goddess), Lord Brahma (the creator), Lord Shiva (the destroyer), and Mother Parvati, among others. Some also include Lord Vishnu, Lord Krishna, and Lord Ram in this list. This raises an important question: Are all these beings God, or are only some of them regarded as such? Can we simply choose any one of them based on personal preference, like selecting items from a buffet?

Interestingly, similar divine personalities are found in many cultures around the world. For example, the Norse god, Thor, known for his thunder and lightning, closely resembles Lord Indra in Vedic tradition, who wields the thunderbolt weapon, *Vajra*. These beings are often seen as responsible for managing specific functions of the universe—for instance, Lord Brahma oversees creation while Lord Shiva manages destruction.

God Is One—Demigods Are His Deputies

Here, it is important to distinguish between God and the demigods. God, by definition, is the Supreme Being. The term "Supreme Being" means the highest entity, beyond whom no one else exists. There can logically be only one Supreme Being. Although the Bhagavad Gita frequently mentions multiple worshippable beings called *devatas* or demigods, it is careful to make a clear distinction between them and the Supreme Lord.

So, who are these demigods? Are they also considered God? According to the Bhagavad Gita, demigods are senior administrators of the universe. They are highly empowered personalities, each managing specific domains such as air, fire, water, rain, and other natural resources that sustain life. From a corporate perspective, they function like departmental heads reporting to the CEO. While powerful, they are not the ultimate authority.

The Supreme Lord, as revealed in the Bhagavad Gita, is the source and controller of all these beings. In Chapter 7, Verse 7, Lord Krishna states: "There is no truth superior to Me. Everything rests upon Me, as pearls are strung on a thread." In Chapter 10, Verse 8, He further clarifies: "I am the source of all spiritual and material worlds. Everything emanates from Me."

When Lord Krishna reveals His Universal Form to Arjuna in Chapter 11, all the demigods are shown as limbs of His cosmic body. In Chapter 10, Verse 2, He emphasizes that even the demigods themselves do not fully understand His origin because He is their source. In simple terms, the demigods are senior executives, but Krishna is the Chairman, the Owner, and the Supreme CEO of the entire cosmic organization.

Each demigod manages a specific aspect of the universe:

- Surya (the Sun god) oversees heat and light.
- Chandra (the God of the Moon) influences vegetation and nourishment.
- Agnidev (the God of fire) controls fire and energy.
- Vayudev (the God of wind and air) governs the movement of air.
- However, all these roles are assigned by the Supreme Lord. They do not operate independently; like departmental heads in a structured organization, they cannot act outside the policies set by the CEO.

The Demigods Depend on the Supreme Lord

This relationship is well-documented in ancient Indian texts like the Srimad Bhagavatam, Ramayana, and Mahabharata. These historical accounts consistently show that when the demigods face problems beyond their control, they turn to the Supreme Lord for assistance. Whether they are overwhelmed by cosmic imbalances, defeated by powerful demons, or unable to manage certain universal challenges, they consistently seek the Supreme Lord's help.

In times of such crises, the Supreme Lord either personally intervenes or sends His empowered representatives to resolve the situation. For instance, when Indra was overpowered by the demon Bali Maharaj, Lord Vishnu, in His Vamana avatar, came to restore cosmic balance. Similarly, when Mother Durga needed strength to defeat the demon Mahishasura, it was the Supreme Lords' combined energy that empowered her. Even Lord Brahma, who is known as the creator of the universe, often seeks guidance and protection from the Supreme Lord.

One of the most significant examples is Lord Shiva, who is often misunderstood as being on par with the Supreme Lord. However, scriptures reveal that Lord Shiva himself prays to Lord Vishnu and Lord Krishna. In the Ramayana, Lord Shiva openly glorifies Lord Ram as the Supreme Personality of Godhead. This demonstrates that even the most powerful demigods ultimately take shelter in the Supreme Lord; they are not His equals, but rather His trusted team members.

While the demigods deserve respect and gratitude for their service in managing the universe, the scriptures consistently guide us to understand the hierarchy. Above all these powerful beings stands the Supreme Lord—the source of everything, the final decision-maker, and the ultimate shelter. Just as in a corporate structure, we can appreciate managers and departmental heads while recognizing that the final authority rests with the CEO, in the grand universal organization, we offer our respect to the demigods, but direct our ultimate devotion to the Supreme Lord.

Just by Worshipping God, All the Demigods are Worshipped

The Vedic literature extensively describes various sacrifices, rituals, and forms of worship directed toward satisfying the demigods. These powerful beings, though highly revered, are ultimately subordinate to the Supreme Lord. Throughout the Bhagavad Gita, the role, position, and purpose of demigods are progressively clarified by Lord Krishna Himself. As we go from one chapter to the next, our understanding deepens regarding how demigod worship is interconnected with the larger system of universal management and the ultimate position of the Supreme Lord.

The concept of demigods is first introduced in the Bhagavad Gita in Chapter 3, where Lord Krishna explains the symbiotic relationship between humans and demigods. In Verse 3.11, He mentions that the Supreme Lord has created an interconnected system in which mankind is meant to perform *yajnas,* or sacrifices, for the satisfaction of the demigods, and in return, the demigods will provide essential necessities such as rain, sunlight, food grains, and other natural resources required for human survival and progress.

This is much like a well-organized enterprise. In any large organization, there are different departments, such as finance, logistics, marketing, and operations, each responsible for specific functions. Similarly, the demigods, headed by personalities like Lord Indra (the controller of rain), Surya (the Sun god), Vayu (the wind god), and many others, are universal administrators managing various resources of creation. If one needs rain, traditionally, one would perform sacrifices for Indra; if one desires good health, worship may be directed toward the Sun god, and so on.

However, Lord Krishna's teachings in the Bhagavad Gita do not stop at simply acknowledging the demigods. In Chapters 7, 9, and 11, Krishna provides a more refined and higher understanding. In Chapter 7, He reveals that all demigod worship ultimately reaches Him, although people may not always realize this. Krishna explains that He is the source of all demigods and that their powers are granted by Him. The demigods are essentially empowered agents, functioning under the supervision of the Supreme Lord, much like regional managers work under the authority of the CEO in a corporate setup.

In Chapter 9, Lord Krishna explicitly states that those who worship demigods are indirectly worshipping Him, but such worship is limited and temporary in its results. Demigod worship may grant specific material benefits, but it does not lead to eternal spiritual advancement. In contrast, direct worship of the Supreme Lord benefits not only the worshipper, but also automatically satisfies all the demigods, since they are parts of His vast universal body and organizational system.

The Srimad Bhagavatam offers two simple yet profound analogies to explain this principle clearly. The first is the analogy of watering the root of a tree. When we pour water on the root, we naturally nourish every branch, leaf, flower, and fruit of the tree. There is no need to water each individual leaf separately. The second analogy compares the Supreme Lord to the stomach of the body. When we provide food to the stomach, all the limbs and organs are automatically energized and satisfied. There is no requirement to feed each part of the body separately.

These analogies emphasize a practical and logical conclusion: when one directly worships the Supreme Lord, all the demigods, who are like various limbs or extensions of His body, are automatically honoured and satisfied. This is because the demigods derive their energies from the Supreme Lord, much like light bulbs derive their illumination from the main power source. Without the power supply, the bulbs have no independent existence or capacity to shine.

Further, the Vedic tradition recognizes the sacred cow, Kamadhenu, as a symbol that embodies all the demigods within her body. Thus, by offering respect to the cow, one pleases all the demigods. Similarly, when we offer our sincere devotion to the Supreme Lord, it is the most inclusive and efficient approach, much like engaging directly with the managing director instead of dealing with each departmental head individually for approvals and resources.

Krishna further elaborates in Chapter 7, Verse 16, that four types of people approach Him: those in distress, those seeking wealth, the inquisitive, and those pursuing knowledge of the Absolute Truth. Interestingly, Lord Krishna does not reject any of them. He graciously accepts all who come to Him, even if their motivations are initially material. He reciprocates with each person according to their desires, gradually elevating them to higher levels of spiritual understanding.

In Chapter 15, Verse 7, Krishna beautifully summarizes that all living beings are His eternal fragments (*amsa*). He is not just the master but also the loving father of all beings. From a relational perspective, it makes more sense to approach one's parents directly for needs rather than going to extended family or acquaintances. Parents naturally care for the welfare of their children and can often provide more comprehensive and lasting support. Similarly, the Supreme Lord, as the ultimate well-wisher, can fulfill all our needs in the most complete way.

Given this perspective, while it is permissible to approach individual demigods for specific requirements, the more intelligent and holistic choice is to worship the Supreme Lord, who is the root of all existence. Not only is this approach simpler, but it is also spiritually progressive because it gradually purifies one's desires and leads to a deeper connection with the Lord.

A thoughtful question arises at this point: When we approach the Supreme Lord, what should we really pray for? Should we ask for temporary benefits, material success, or relief from distress? Or should we aim for something higher? The Bhagavad Gita gently guides us toward higher aspirations that go beyond mere material gains. It encourages us to seek eternal shelter, spiritual knowledge, and ultimately pure love for the Supreme Lord.

This is a deeper subject that we will explore later in this book. For now, it is important to recognize that while demigod worship is part of a larger universal system, direct devotion to the Supreme Lord is the most comprehensive, effective, and spiritually rewarding path. By understanding this, we can make informed choices about whom to approach, what to ask for, and how to align our spiritual practices with the highest purpose of life.

CHAPTER 9

GOD - AN EVIL DICTATOR, OR OUR BEST FRIEND?

God, Suffering, and the Erroneous Conclusion: Why the All-Good, All-Powerful God Still Makes Sense

In the previous chapters, we explored the existence of God from various perspectives—common sense, philosophical reasoning, scientific consideration, and scriptural evidence. After examining these multiple dimensions, we arrived at a coherent conclusion: God is a person, not some abstract force, and among all personalities, He is the most attractive, the Supreme Being, the reservoir of all pleasure and beauty. We also established that God is one, not many, and that no individual entity can be equated with God. There is a unique Supreme Personality of Godhead who is distinct from the multitude of living entities.

However, one particularly challenging argument remains to be addressed—a question that has perplexed philosophers, spiritual seekers, and everyday people alike for centuries: If God exists and if He is all-powerful and all-good, why is there so much suffering in this world? Why do innocent people suffer? Why is life often so cruel? These questions are not just an academic curiosity, but deeply personal ones that arise, especially in moments of pain and helplessness.

Renowned author Harold Kushner, in his book *When Bad Things Happen to Good People,* poignantly posed this dilemma. He suggested that perhaps God can either be all-good or all-powerful but not both—otherwise, how can the existence of suffering be explained? If God is loving, then maybe He lacks the power to stop suffering. Or if He is powerful, then perhaps He is not fully benevolent. This faulty conclusion, though emotionally compelling, requires deeper inspection.

To help us understand the flaw in this logic, let us consider a simple story:

The Barber's Illusion: A Story of Misunderstood Logic

Once, there was an atheist barber who frequently shared his atheistic ideas with customers while cutting their hair. One day, a devotee of the Lord visited the barber's shop for a haircut. As the barber went about his work, he confidently proclaimed: "Look at the world around us. People are suffering everywhere. If there truly was a God who is omnipotent and compassionate, why would He allow so much pain? Clearly, God does not exist."

The devotee listened patiently without immediate argument. After the haircut, he left the shop but soon returned, pointing out a group of people outside with long, unkempt hair and untrimmed beards.

"Barbers do not exist," the devotee told the barber.

The barber, startled, replied, "What do you mean? I am standing right here. Of course barbers exist. If those people with long hair came to me, I would certainly groom them."

The devotee smiled and responded, "Exactly. God exists, too. It is just that those who suffer often do not approach Him. If they sought shelter in God, they would certainly experience His grace, and their suffering would diminish."

This simple analogy exposes the flaw in assuming that God's presence automatically eliminates suffering without any voluntary engagement on our part. Just as a barber cannot cut the hair of someone who refuses to come to his shop, God does not forcibly impose His shelter on those who do not seek it.

God: The Perfect Parent, Not the Pampering Parent

This leads us to an essential question: Is God a cruel, indifferent ruler who enjoys the suffering of His children, or is there a more nuanced understanding we might be missing?

The Vedic scriptures reveal that each soul is an infinitesimal part of God—a spark of His energy. This understanding raises an important question: Why would an all-powerful, all-loving father allow His children to undergo painful experiences?

To reflect on this, let us consider the example of a parent-child relationship. What makes a parent truly ideal? Is it the parent who blindly satisfies every whim and desire of their child—letting the child play all day, eat only sweets, and skip school? To a child, such parents may initially seem perfect. However, any responsible adult would recognize that this kind of parenting would eventually lead to disaster. The child's future would be ruined, their potential unfulfilled, and they would suffer greatly as they grow up lacking essential life skills and discipline.

Conversely, parents who sometimes say "no", who set boundaries, and who discipline their children with love and firm guidance are actually the ones who provide the best long-term care. Such parents are committed to their child's true well-being, not just their immediate happiness.

Similarly, God is the Perfect Parent. He does not exist simply to indulge our short-term desires. Rather, His concern is for our ultimate benefit. He arranges circumstances—including hardships—to guide us towards growth, rectification, and the eternal happiness of reconnecting with Him.

From this perspective, suffering is not evidence of God's absence or cruelty; it is evidence of His careful supervision and deep concern for the evolution of each soul.

The Laws of Karma: God's Supreme Justice System

To understand why different people experience varying degrees of happiness and suffering, we need a system that is consistent, impartial, and universally applicable. The concept of karma—explained extensively in the Bhagavad Gita—provides this framework.

The law of karma is essentially the universal system of action and reaction: "As you sow, so shall you reap." This principle operates much like the judicial systems of modern nations, where actions are linked to consequences, both rewards and punishments. Just as a country without a legal framework would descend into chaos and disorder, the universe operates under a system of divine law and order, meticulously governed by karma.

Importantly, this system is perfectly managed by God, who is neutral and just. His laws are not influenced by partiality, bribery, or error. Karma explains why individuals are born into different circumstances—some with apparent advantages and others with significant challenges.

Why is someone born into wealth, while another is born into poverty? Why is one child naturally gifted in music or science, while another struggles? Karma provides the answer. Current life circumstances are not random or unfair; they are the results of our own past choices, not just in this life, but over countless previous lives.

This explanation is far more comprehensive than simply attributing suffering to genetics, brain chemistry, or social inequalities. Yes, medical science may observe neurotransmitter imbalances in depression, but the question remains: Why does that imbalance manifest in one individual and not another? Karma goes deeper—it addresses the root causes that extend beyond a single lifetime.

God: The Impartial Judge and Our Greatest Well-Wisher

It is essential to understand that pain, from a spiritual perspective, is not intended to torment, but to reform. The judicial systems of the world ideally exist to rehabilitate, not simply punish. Similarly, the pain and suffering we experience are corrective measures designed to steer us back toward our true path.

God is like a Supreme Judge. He does not arbitrarily send pleasure to some and pain to others. His judgements are based on the infallible law of karma, and He remains neutral in delivering the outcomes of our own choices. Just as the GPS in our smartphones constantly recalculates the best route regardless of how many wrong turns we make, God continually offers us opportunities to correct our course, no matter how far we may have strayed.

Through these life experiences, especially the painful ones, we are nudged to ask deeper questions: Who am I? Why am I here? What is the true purpose of life? Pain propels us to seek solutions, to question material existence, and eventually to search for God.

Interestingly, our entire life's activity—whether we realize it or not—is centred around two fundamental pursuits: the quest for happiness and the desire to be free from suffering. Every decision we make and every effort we undertake ultimately serves these two goals.

What scriptures like the Bhagavad Gita reveal is that true and lasting happiness, as well as complete freedom from suffering, can only be attained by re-establishing our loving relationship with God. While temporary pleasures may seem satisfying, they inevitably fade, and new pains arise. Only a spiritual connection offers sustainable joy.

God is not a distant judge; He is our ever-well-wisher, a loving father, and a compassionate friend who walks alongside us, gently guiding us back toward Him. Even when we repeatedly make mistakes and deviate from the optimal path, He persistently recalculates the route—much like the GPS—always ready to guide us toward our ultimate destination.

However, the key is that we must choose to stay connected. The GPS only works if the device remains switched on. Similarly, our relationship with God flourishes when we make the effort to remain spiritually connected through prayer, meditation, sincere enquiry, and selfless service.

Reframing the Dilemma: God's Justice and Love Go Hand-in-Hand

The age-old question of suffering need not be a spiritual dead end. When we understand the depth of God's system and His parental care, the apparent contradiction dissolves. God's power and goodness coexist perfectly. His governance is fair, meticulous, and deeply loving. The suffering in this world is not an indication of God's absence, but a reflection of His profound commitment to our growth and ultimate happiness.

We can appreciate this better when we realize that this material world is not our permanent home. It is a training ground, a reformatory, a temporary station in our eternal journey. The ultimate goal is to transcend this cycle of birth and death and return to the spiritual realm, where there is no suffering and no temporary happiness—only an uninterrupted loving exchange with God.

In the corporate world, when an employee is assigned challenging tasks, it is not always a sign of punishment; often, it is a sign of trust, an opportunity to grow and develop higher capacities. Similarly, the challenges we face in life are tailored experiences designed to help us realize our true potential as spiritual beings.

Ultimately, the solution is not to accuse God of injustice, but to take personal responsibility for our lives, to understand the principles of karma, and to embrace the opportunity to reconnect with God, who is not only supremely powerful, but also supremely compassionate.

Like a caring parent, God patiently waits for us to turn toward Him. And when we do, we discover that His door has always been open.

CHAPTER 10

WHY DO BAD THINGS HAPPEN TO GOOD PEOPLE, AND VICE VERSA?

From Pain to Purpose – The Spiritual Audit Trail

One of the most difficult and frustrating questions that even the sharpest minds struggle to answer is: **Why do bad things happen to good people?** You see a kind-hearted person battling illness, a generous soul facing betrayal, or a disciplined individual losing everything overnight, and the natural reaction is: "It's not fair."

That's because deep down, we believe that goodness should be rewarded. We expect life to function like a well-managed company: input sincerity, output success. However, as we know from experience, life doesn't always follow our logic. So, where's the disconnect?

To truly understand this, we need to step away from emotional impulses and look at the larger design of the universe—not just materially, but spiritually.

The World Is Not a Paradise—It's a Correctional Facility

In some progressive countries, prisons are no longer called jails but rather correctional centres or rehabilitation facilities. The idea is simple: the purpose of the sentence is not punishment alone, but reform.

Similarly, from a spiritual perspective—especially in the Vedic understanding—the material world is not a pleasure park but a **corrective centre for the soul**. It is a place where living beings go through various experiences—some pleasant, some painful—that are required to reform, reflect, and eventually return to their original pure state.

The world is not meant to be perfect. The Bhagavad Gita describes it as "*dukhalayam asasvatam*"—a place of misery and temporariness. However, the purpose behind that design is not cruelty; it's correction. Just as a fever is not the problem but a symptom helping you detect a deeper issue, **pain serves as the universe's wake-up call**.

Pain Initiates the Audit Trail

We don't generally pause during pleasurable times. However, pain makes us stop and reflect.

Consider this: What prompts most people to ask the deeper questions of life? It's not a promotion or a vacation; it's often a personal setback, heartbreak, loss, or health scare. It is suffering that triggers introspection. This pattern is found not only in scriptures, but also in real life.

This is the **audit trail of transformation**:

1. **Pain leads to enquiry.**
   - "Why is this happening to me?"
   - "Is there any meaning to this life?"
   - "What is my purpose?"

   These questions often arise in a crisis, not in comfort.

2. **Enquiry leads to knowledge.**
   The more you question sincerely, the more life (or God) connects you to answers—through books, mentors, saints, or spiritual communities.
3. **Knowledge leads to purification.**
   As the fog lifts, we begin to see clearly—our habits, attachments, mistakes, and desires. This clarity is the beginning of transformation.
4. **Purification leads to liberation.**
   Eventually, we outgrow the need for repeated suffering, just as a student graduates and no longer needs to return to the same classroom.

In other words, **pain is not the end of the story; it is the beginning of awakening.**

Karma: The Invisible Justice System

To understand why suffering seems to come even to good people, we need to understand the law of **karma**—the universal system of cause and effect.

Every action creates a reaction. Just as physical laws, like gravity, apply to everyone regardless of belief, **karma applies impartially** to all living beings. What we do, consciously or unconsciously, sets into motion consequences that may manifest immediately, after some time, or even in a future life.

It's crucial to note that **not all karmic consequences are visible in this life.** For instance, someone who appears saintly in behaviour and still suffers today might be facing the results of a past life misdeed. Conversely, someone seemingly corrupt may be enjoying good karma from past actions that haven't yet run out.

If we only look at one frame in a long movie, things might seem out of order. However, once you zoom out, the storyline makes sense. Karma is that zoomed-out view. It explains the present based on the unseen past and determines the future through the choices we make now.

Is There a Way Out of Suffering?

Yes—and that's the good news.

Just as good behaviour in a correctional centre can lead to early release or rehabilitation, spiritual practices offer a way to reduce and eventually eliminate karmic suffering.

Ancient texts mention four types of sinful reactions:

1. ***Aprarabdha*** – Dormant, not yet manifested
2. ***Bijam*** – In seed form
3. ***Kutam*** – Sprouting stage
4. ***Prarabdha*** – Already bearing fruit

All four types of reactions can be neutralized through Yoga, more specifically through Bhakti Yoga.

The Bhagavad Gita states:

"Aham tvam sarva-papebhyo mokshayishyami ma sucah" (18.66)
"I shall deliver you from all sinful reactions. Do not fear."

This isn't just poetic; it's a powerful truth. The moment we reconnect with the Divine in love and service, our karmic baggage begins to burn, and a new path unfolds.

Why Do Good People Still Suffer?

There are several reasons:

1. **They Are Burning Off Past Karma**
   Even a saint may carry a heavy load of previous actions. Suffering is not unjust; it's like a loan being paid off.
2. **They Are Being Prepared for Greater Responsibility**
   Just as diamonds are cut with pressure, the Lord sometimes tests sincere souls to refine them. These tests are not retribution, but qualification.

3. **They Accept Voluntary Suffering to Help Others**
   Some spiritually advanced souls take on hardship as part of their service to uplift humanity, just like doctors who volunteer in disaster zones.

4. **They Are Getting Their Education Fast-tracked**
   Sometimes, suffering acts as an accelerator. It breaks comfort zones and promotes rapid growth—mentally, emotionally, and spiritually.

What Can We Do Practically?

Even with all this understanding, when suffering occurs, the pain is real. Here's how to respond—not just react:

1. **Accept the Bigger Picture**
   Don't get stuck in the "Why me?" spiral. Trust that there's a larger design at work—even if it's not immediately visible.

2. **Pause and Reflect**
   Use pain as a signal, not an enemy. Ask what this situation is trying to teach you. Write, meditate, or speak to wise individuals.

3. **Take Responsibility, Not Blame**
   There's a difference. Blame weakens you, while responsibility empowers you to change what can be changed—your response, choices, and mindset.

4. **Engage in Spiritual Practices**
   Acts like prayer, *mantra* meditation (like chanting the *Hare Krishna maha-mantra*), reading wisdom texts, or serving others elevate our consciousness and help us move beyond suffering.

5. **Avoid Actions that Create Future Karma**
   The Vedic texts outline four primary sinful pillars:

- Eating non-vegetarian food
- Intoxication
- Gambling
- Illicit sex

Avoiding these not only prevents future negative reactions, but also brings immediate mental clarity.

The Soul Doesn't Suffer – It Just Identifies with the Suffering Mind

Here's the final insight: **you are not your body or mind—you are the soul.** The body may experience pain, and the mind may encounter confusion, but the soul remains untouched. Just as a person watching a movie may feel emotions, but is not actually in danger, the soul witnesses the body's experiences. The goal of life is to remember this identity and live in harmony with it.

When we anchor ourselves in the soul, in our spiritual identity, and in our relationship with the Supreme Lord, we find **strength in storms**, **clarity in confusion**, and **hope even in hardship**.

Conclusion: From Suffering to Spiritual Success

So, do bad things happen to good people?

Yes, but not without reason, purpose, or the possibility of transformation.

Every painful moment can either harden us or awaken us; the choice is ours. When we view this world not as a battleground of fairness versus injustice, but as a **correctional centre for the soul**, life begins to make sense. In this context, **pain is not the enemy; it is the teacher.** Once we pass the exam, we graduate from difficulty and the entire cycle of birth and death.

CHAPTER 11

LESSONS FROM THE TITANIC AND COVID

The Urgent Need for Reflection

In today's hyper-connected, relentlessly fast-paced world, the ability to think clearly and make meaningful decisions is becoming increasingly rare. We are constantly on the move—managing deadlines, chasing targets, and firefighting daily operational demands. In this continuous cycle of activity, genuine introspection—the kind that drives personal growth, strategic clarity, and long-term fulfillment—often takes a back seat. Yet, it is precisely this kind of deep, conscious reflection that is critical for recalibrating our lives and aligning our actions with our core values and purpose.

To achieve this, we must deliberately carve out time and mental space away from the noise of our busy schedules. This requires us to step into environments that promote stillness and focus, away from the persistent pings of notifications and the pressures of immediate deliverables. Only when we pause and intentionally declutter our minds can we begin to assess honestly where we currently stand and whether we are genuinely progressing towards a purposeful and impactful life.

Unfortunately, the modern corporate and social environment seems to reward perpetual busyness. Many professionals find themselves caught in a treadmill of activities—not necessarily because they are adding significant value, but simply to keep pace or maintain a perceived standard of success. Comfort and survival have silently become the new benchmarks, replacing the pursuit of meaning and excellence. The real tragedy is that most people rarely, if ever, step back to evaluate whether the life they are building aligns with their deeper goals and aspirations. Few realize the magnitude of the precarious situation we all face—a life potentially spent in motion without true direction or fulfillment. Making time for reflection is no longer a luxury; it is an urgent necessity for anyone seeking authentic success and sustainable well-being.

Our Real Position in This World

Let's take a moment to step back, put on our thinking hats, and evaluate the big picture. What is our actual position in this world? Occasionally, life forces us to face this question—when an unexpected tragedy strikes, when we lose a loved one, or when a serious challenge arises at work, in our health, or in our closest relationships.

In such moments, people briefly pause. The busyness of life temporarily halts, and for a short while, we ponder the unexpected turn of events, trying to grasp the shock of reality. Many questions arise: Why me? Why now? What is the meaning of all this? Unfortunately, more often than not, these questions are either suppressed or answered superficially, as we rarely seek answers in the right places.

Well-wishers typically comfort us with the familiar phrase, "This too shall pass." While some people manage to move on, others continue to struggle under the weight of their circumstances, and a few even collapse under the pressure. This approach might bring temporary relief, but it rarely provides lasting clarity or meaningful solutions.

Some motivational voices in society advocate an attitude of relentless optimism: "It doesn't matter what life throws at you—just keep batting." They compare life to a cricket match, where you face good balls, bad balls, and the occasional googly. They say, "Stay positive. Don't be a pessimist."

While this sounds encouraging, there's value in being realistically optimistic rather than blindly hopeful. It's important to confront life's challenges and uncertainties head-on and proactively seek sustainable solutions instead of ignoring life's challenges, sugarcoating reality, or pretending that everything will somehow work out on its own. Simply put, it's better to light a candle than to sit and complain about the darkness.

The Inescapable Uncertainty of Life

The hard, undeniable truth is that life can turn upside down at any moment, without warning, and it can happen to anyone in any aspect of life. Whether in our career, relationships, physical health, mental well-being, finances, social standing, or even the political climate around us, no area is immune to sudden disruption. Natural disasters, corporate fraud, unexpected health diagnoses, and economic recessions—the list is long and unending.

This unpredictability does not discriminate; it applies to everyone—rich and poor, young and old, people of all races and nationalities. No one is exempt from life's uncertainties.

Lessons from the Titanic

The tragic sinking of the Titanic serves as a powerful example of this reality. The Titanic was marketed as the pinnacle of luxury, engineering, and safety. It was equipped with everything that symbolized human advancement and opulence: a gymnasium, swimming pool, fine dining restaurants, high-end cafes, Turkish baths, and cutting-edge communication systems. It had watertight compartments and remotely controlled safety doors. It was considered "unsinkable".

Yet, the ship sank on its very first voyage.

The Titanic carried millionaires, aristocrats, middle-class passengers, labourers, and even animals—none of whom were spared by the disaster. Interestingly, among the many animals onboard, only three dogs survived.

Was this just a tragic accident, or was there a deeper force at play? The Titanic's story is a sobering reminder that no matter how strong, secure, or sophisticated our position may seem, in the vast ocean of life, we are all as vulnerable as a matchbox floating on water.

Some may argue that the Titanic disaster was a once-in-a-century event, but that's not entirely accurate. History is full of similar catastrophes—other shipwrecks, natural calamities, nuclear disasters, economic collapses, and more. Life consistently proves that no matter how powerful or well-prepared we think we are, we are constantly operating in a highly unpredictable environment.

Lessons from the Covid-19 Pandemic

More recently, the Covid-19 pandemic served as a global reality check. It did not spare anyone; entire nations, both developed and developing, were brought to their knees. Regardless of wealth, status, race, nationality, or religion, the virus affected people indiscriminately. The pandemic triggered widespread loss—not only in terms of life, but also in mental health, economic stability, and social connectivity.

Even now, despite vaccines and improved medical interventions, the world is not entirely safe from Covid-like threats. If we have learned anything, it is that disease continues to evolve, and despite medical advancements, there are still countless illnesses with no effective cures. The increasing specialization in modern medicine—where doctors focus on specific body parts—is, in itself, an indication that the body is prone to an ever-expanding range of ailments.

Yes, medical technology has advanced significantly, but diseases and disorders continue to emerge, many of which are resistant to treatment. Some futurists may claim that one day, science will conquer death or allow us to transfer human consciousness into digital or robotic bodies. This sounds exciting and ambitious. However, Srila Prabhupada, the founder of the International Society for Krishna Consciousness (ISKCON), cautioned that such promises are like post-dated cheques. They may seem valuable now, but they offer no actual solution for the present.

There's a famous English proverb: "Trust no future, however pleasant it may appear." The present reality remains uncertain, and that is the sober truth.

Some people might ask, "What's the point of dwelling on all this? We just have to keep finding solutions for our problems and be prepared for those we can't solve." Others say that life's difficulties are necessary to help us appreciate happiness when it comes. But if that's true, why do we instinctively try to avoid suffering at all costs? Why do we continuously develop technologies, policies, and personal strategies to escape pain and misfortune?

This contradiction highlights the need for a deeper enquiry.

Diagnosing the Root Cause

The Vedic scriptures offer profound insights into the nature of life. There's a well-known Bengali verse: "*Kamala jala dala, jivana tala mala*," which means, this life is as unsteady as a drop of water on a lotus leaf. A slight breeze, and everything is gone.

We can be perfectly healthy today and face a life-threatening illness tomorrow. We can be extremely wealthy one day and find ourselves bankrupt the next. Relationships that seem solid can deteriorate overnight. Mental well-being can quickly spiral into depression. Life can change dramatically in a matter of moments.

So, what's the takeaway? Simply saying, "This too shall pass" may offer momentary relief, but it does not constitute real intelligence. True wisdom lies in identifying the root cause of life's challenges and searching for sustainable, meaningful solutions—not just surface-level bandages.

Recognizing our inherent vulnerability is not a pessimistic worldview; it's simply an honest acknowledgement of the reality of our existence. Denial is not a strategy. Facing the truth and preparing for it is the foundation of resilience.

Understanding the true diagnosis of life is a significant step toward effective problem-solving. As the saying goes, a correct diagnosis is half the cure. The other half lies in addressing the root cause, not in superficial, temporary fixes.

The Bhagavad Gita and other timeless spiritual texts emphasize this fundamental point. The root cause of our suffering is not external events; it stems from our deep identification with the temporary, ever-changing material world.

We pursue positions, possessions, and pleasures, mistaking them to be our ultimate security. However, the material world is inherently temporary, uncertain, and filled with dualities.

Once we accept this reality, we can begin to seek solutions that go beyond mere patchwork remedies. We can transition from reactive living to proactive understanding. This is the pathway to true wisdom and inner stability.

There is a deeper, more sustainable solution, which begins with changing our understanding of who we are, why we are here, and what the ultimate purpose of life is.

Stay tuned.

CHAPTER 12

THE MATRIX OF THIS WORLD

The Matrix Movie Series and Its Storyline

Practically everyone has, at some point, heard about or watched *The Matrix* movie series, directed by the Wachowski siblings. While the first film in the series was widely acclaimed and well-received by global audiences, very few people truly understood the deeper mystical themes and philosophical intricacies embedded within its plot. On the surface, it appears to be a highly engaging science fiction thriller, packed with groundbreaking special effects and intense action sequences. However, when examined more closely, *The Matrix* is much more than just entertainment—it's a deep metaphorical commentary on reality, illusion, and the human condition.

In simple terms, the storyline revolves around the concept of a simulated reality. In the movie, the term "Matrix" refers to a virtual world of illusion—a computer-generated environment that appears completely real to the individuals trapped within it. This illusory world is so convincingly designed that most people are unaware that they are living in a simulation. In the real world, their physical bodies are depicted as being in a state of suspended animation, while their consciousness is fully engaged in the virtual Matrix. Human beings unknowingly live their entire lives in this illusory construct, firmly believing that what they are experiencing is reality.

However, a small group of individuals inside the Matrix comes to realize the shocking truth—the world they believe to be real is, in fact, an elaborate deception. Determined to break free, they embark on a mission to escape the Matrix and help others liberate themselves from the illusion. The hero of the story, Neo, undergoes a transformative journey of self-discovery, ultimately acquiring the ability to see the Matrix for what it truly is—a complex web of binary code, bits, and bytes projected as tangible reality. This moment of realization serves as the turning point in the first movie and sets the stage for a much deeper philosophical exploration in the sequels. *The Matrix* series, therefore, is not merely about science fiction; it is a brilliant narrative that prompts viewers to question the nature of reality itself.

The Matrix and the Bhagavad Gita: A Striking Parallel

What makes *The Matrix* even more fascinating is its remarkable resemblance to the timeless wisdom of the Bhagavad Gita, one of India's most revered spiritual texts. In the Bhagavad Gita, Lord Krishna reveals to Arjuna a profound and captivating secret: the existence of two distinct worlds. One is the material world we currently inhabit—a realm composed of matter, which is temporary, illusory, and filled with dualities like pleasure and pain. The other is the spiritual world—a dimension made of anti-matter or pure spirit, which is eternal, blissful, and free from the limitations of birth, death, and suffering.

Lord Krishna explains that the material world is inherently a place of misery. It is a temporary realm, continuously moving through cycles of creation, maintenance, and destruction. In contrast, the spiritual world is described as a permanent reality, where happiness is ever-increasing and there is no fear of loss or decay. The Bhagavad Gita urges human beings to awaken from their illusions—much like the characters in *The Matrix*—and to strive towards realizing the spiritual reality that exists beyond the material façade.

The parallels between *The Matrix* and the Bhagavad Gita are striking and thought-provoking. Both present a scenario where most people unknowingly accept an illusory world as reality, while only a few courageous souls question it and seek the truth. Both convey the message that true freedom lies in knowledge, self-awareness, and breaking free from deception.

In a world increasingly driven by surface-level distractions and artificial experiences, these insights serve as a powerful reminder to look deeper and search for what is truly real.

The Choice is Ours to Make – Blue Pill or Red Pill?

In the groundbreaking movie *The Matrix*, the central theme revolves around the concept of choice—the opportunity to embrace reality or continue living in a comforting illusion. The mission of the people in the real world, particularly the team led by Morpheus, is to rescue others from the Matrix and introduce them to the truth. Morpheus, one of the most pivotal characters, offers a life-defining choice to those still trapped in the Matrix: two pills—one blue and one red. The choice is both simple and profound. By taking the blue pill, one opts to remain in ignorance, continuing life within the illusory confines of the Matrix, blissfully unaware of the deeper reality. On the other hand, by taking the red pill, one chooses to awaken to a new and often uncomfortable truth, stepping out of the illusion and into the real world. The red pill represents the willingness to face a difficult, life-altering reality, while the blue pill signifies a decision to stay within the comfort zone of familiar but ultimately false perceptions.

Interestingly, this concept closely parallels the profound philosophical teachings of the Bhagavad Gita that address the very same human dilemma, albeit in a different context. In the Bhagavad Gita, Lord Krishna offers us a similar crossroads. The blue pill equivalent is to remain absorbed in the temporary, ever-changing material world—a world that, although it may appear attractive, ultimately brings frustration, suffering, and disappointment. People in this world continuously strive for happiness, yet lasting satisfaction always seems just out of reach. This illusion keeps them trapped, much like the characters in *The Matrix*, believing that fulfillment lies somewhere within the material framework.

Conversely, In the Bhagavad Gita, Lord Krishna, through Arjuna, presents us with the red pill option—to courageously recognize that true happiness can never be attained in the material world, no matter how hard we try. Instead, we are encouraged to redirect our efforts toward the spiritual realm, the eternal world beyond birth, death, disease, and old age. The Bhagavad Gita emphasizes that this transformative journey—from illusion to reality—is made possible through the process of Yoga. Yoga, in its deepest sense, is not just a physical discipline but a complete lifestyle and mindset focused on connecting the individual soul with the Supreme Divine. It provides the practical tools and frameworks to elevate our consciousness, make informed choices, and gradually transition from material entanglement to spiritual freedom.

Ultimately, the choice remains ours. Do we continue to accept the surface-level narrative offered by the material world, or do we dig deeper to uncover a higher purpose and a more fulfilling reality? In a world driven by speed, ambition, and temporary pleasures, very few pause to reflect on these choices. But for those who do, the red pill path offers not just an alternative perspective—it offers the doorway to genuine happiness, enduring peace, and a life of purpose that transcends fleeting successes. The question is, are we ready to make that choice?

Welcome to the Real World

"Welcome to the real world," says Morpheus as Neo finally awakens from the dream-like existence of the Matrix and finds himself in the harsh, unfiltered reality. This is a pivotal moment in the movie, marking Neo's transition from illusion to truth, from ignorance to awareness. However, before Morpheus delivers this profound statement, an intense and meaningful dialogue takes place—one that sets the tone for the rest of the movie and carries deep philosophical weight. Let's take a moment to revisit that conversation, as it carries striking parallels to our own lives and the timeless teachings of the Bhagavad Gita.

When Morpheus first meets Neo within the Matrix—the illusory world that Neo has always assumed to be real—he immediately offers him a choice: the famous blue pill or red pill. Their conversation unfolds as follows:

Morpheus: *"At last. Welcome, Neo. As you no doubt have guessed, I am Morpheus."*

Neo: *"It's an honour to meet you."*

Morpheus: *"No, the honour is mine. Please, come. Sit. I imagine that right now you're feeling a bit like Alice tumbling down the rabbit hole?"*

Neo: *"You could say that."*

Morpheus: *"I can see it in your eyes. You have the look of a man who accepts what he sees because he's expecting to wake up. Ironically, this is not far from the truth. Let me tell you why you're here. You know something. What you know, you can't explain, but you feel it. You've felt it your entire life. Something's wrong with the world. You don't know what it is, but it's there. Like a splinter in your mind, driving you mad. It is this feeling that has brought you to me. Do you know what I'm talking about?"*

Neo: *"The Matrix?"*

Morpheus: *"Do you want to know what it is? The Matrix is everywhere. It is all around us. Even now, in this very room. You can see it when you look out your window or when you turn on your television. You can feel it when you go to work, when you go to church, when you pay your taxes. It is the world that has been pulled over your eyes to blind you from the truth."*

Neo: *"What truth?"*

Morpheus: *"That you are a slave. Like everyone else, you were born into bondage, born into a prison that you cannot smell or taste or touch. A prison for your mind. Unfortunately, no one can be told what the Matrix is. You have to see it for yourself. This is your last chance. After this, there is no turning back. You take the blue pill, the story ends, you wake up in your bed and believe whatever you want to believe. You take the red pill, you stay in Wonderland,*

and I show you how deep the rabbit hole goes. Remember, all I'm offering is the truth. Nothing more."
Neo, driven by a relentless desire to understand the truth, chooses the red pill.

Morpheus: *"Follow me."*

This moment in the movie is not just cinematic brilliance; it is profoundly symbolic. The choice offered to Neo is essentially the same choice each one of us faces in life: Do we continue living in comfortable ignorance, accepting the world as it is presented to us, or do we dare to pursue the inconvenient truths that may completely dismantle our current understanding of reality?

This theme deeply resonates with the eternal wisdom of the Bhagavad Gita. Just as Morpheus explains that something is fundamentally wrong with the world—a feeling Neo has harboured but could never articulate—we, too, sense that something isn't quite right with our own lives. In our quieter moments of reflection, especially during times of distress, we often experience a sense of dissatisfaction, a subtle but persistent realization that no matter how hard we try, happiness seems elusive. The temporary pleasures we chase are often fleeting, while pain and dissatisfaction tend to linger.

The Bhagavad Gita profoundly addresses this condition of human life. Lord Krishna describes this material world as "*dukhalayam ashashvatam*"—a place of misery, filled with temporary and fleeting experiences. Just as we refer to a *vidyalaya* as a place where knowledge is acquired or a *bhojanalaya* as a place where food is served, *dukhalaya* signifies a world where suffering is guaranteed. Regardless of who we are—our nationality, profession, wealth, or social status—misery remains an inseparable aspect of life here.

In the modern corporate environment, we often dress up this suffering with polished terms like stress management, work-life balance, and mental health initiatives. Yet, beneath the surface, dissatisfaction persists. No amount of career success, social recognition, or financial security seems to provide lasting fulfillment. In *The Matrix*, this was the illusion—the belief that material achievements equate to freedom. In reality, as Morpheus highlights, it's a sophisticated form of slavery.

The Bhagavad Gita offers a path to break free from this invisible bondage. It invites us, much like Morpheus did, to question our assumptions, introspect, and take the metaphorical red pill—the pursuit of transcendental knowledge. It encourages us to look beyond the superficial layers of life and understand the deeper spiritual truths that govern our existence.

Ultimately, just as Neo's journey commences after he chooses truth over comfort, our journey toward real freedom and happiness begins when we confront the deeper realities of life. The choice is before us: do we take the blue pill and remain comfortably distracted, or do we take the red pill and step into the real world?

Prisoners by Choice

Just as Morpheus states that everyone in the Matrix was born into bondage, the Bhagavad Gita describes the material world we currently inhabit as a prison—a reformation house for souls. In such a prison, shackles must exist, and here, those shackles take the form of attachments to the objects and people of this world. As long as we cling to even a single thing, whether animate or inanimate, we remain here and suffer birth after birth. It is only when a Guru or spiritual master enters our lives, enlightens us about the reality of this world and our real identity as the soul, and informs us about the perfect spiritual world along with the process to transition, that we can transcend this miserable existence. Just like a fish that is out of water cannot be happy even when placed in first-class milk or provided with all the comforts of life; we, the living spirit souls, cannot find joy through the various comforts afforded to our gross and subtle bodies in this world. However, just by returning to water or being thrown back into it by the fisherman, the fish will again become happy. In the same way, the spirit soul will attain happiness by entering the spiritual world, the real world.

Characteristics of the Real World

What are some characteristics of the spiritual world—the real world—as described in Vedic literature, including the Bhagavad Gita? It is mentioned that the spiritual world is eternal, full of knowledge, and overflowing with bliss. Among other differences, five truths which exist in the material world are non-existent in the spiritual realm, collectively referred to as *pavarga. Pavarga* corresponds to the Sanskrit letters *pa, fa, ba, bha*, and *ma*.

- *Pa* refers to *parisrama*, signifying that everyone must work hard in this world to maintain themselves.
- *Fa* refers to *fena* or foam, indicating that everyone must work so hard that foam forms at their mouths.
- *Ba* refers to *bandhan* or bondage, which means that everyone is bound in this world and cannot escape its miseries.
- *Bha* refers to *bhaya* or fear, which exists in every sphere and moment of our lives due to the harsh reality that anything can happen to anyone at any time. There is no absolute security, even if we equip ourselves with the best forms of security, like bank balances, family, friends, contacts,

insurance policies, and more. We experience a variety of fears regarding our health, careers, relationships, and the well-being of our loved ones.

- *Ma* refers to *mrityu,* or death, which marks the end of a chapter in our lives. The saying "As sure as death" encapsulates the inevitability of mortality: every person who is born must eventually die. Throughout history, many powerful individuals have existed but have ultimately returned to dust. At the moment of death, everything we possess and are attached to is forcibly taken away from us, or rather, we are taken away from all of them.

In contrast, the spiritual world is described as *apavarga* or a place where these five miseries do not exist. In the spiritual world, no one has to forcibly work hard to maintain their lives. There is no bondage—everyone is free in all respects. There is absolutely no fear, and complete security prevails. Finally, there is no death, only an eternal life filled with bliss.

As Morpheus says, all we are offering is the truth. Nothing more, nothing less.

Welcome to the Real World!

CHAPTER 13

MULTIVERSE IN THE VEDAS AND BEYOND

The Concept of Multiverse in Modern and Ancient Thought

A fascinating article recently appeared on www.newscientist.com, titled "We are closer than ever to finally proving the multiverse exists." In this article, journalist Miriam Frankel makes a bold statement:

"One hundred years ago, we discovered there were other galaxies beyond our own. Now, we might be on the verge of another discovery: that there are other universes."

This highlights how rapidly our understanding of the cosmos is evolving. Earlier, people believed the Milky Way was the entirety of the universe. However, scientists later discovered that billions of galaxies exist beyond our own. Now, they are considering whether even this vast universe of ours might be just one among many others—a concept known as the Multiverse.

Frankel goes on to say that there could be many ways these other universes exist. Some might have been born just after the Big Bang, while others may be hiding in extra dimensions. Some might pop into existence when a quantum possibility turns into reality. Each universe may adhere to different laws, different constants, or even a different reality altogether. Some may resemble ours closely, while others could be entirely unrecognizable.

Is the Multiverse a New Idea?

You might think this is a brand-new theory, but the concept of multiple universes is actually ancient. Philosophers from Greece—like Anaximander and Democritus—spoke of many worlds long ago. In fact, for centuries, the notion of "many universes" has appeared in both philosophical and spiritual texts across the world.

Over time, the multiverse idea has made its way into several fields, from science and cosmology to philosophy and science fiction. While some scientists embrace it, others remain cautious because, so far, there is no solid experimental proof to support it. It's not easy to find physical evidence of other universes, especially if they are completely separate from our own. Nonetheless, the idea continues to spark imagination and debate.

Some scientists believe that the multiverse theory could help resolve problems in physics—like explaining why the laws of nature are so perfectly tuned for life. Others argue it's more of a philosophical or mathematical concept than a strictly scientific one because we don't yet have tools to observe or test it.

What Exactly Is the Multiverse?

In his book *The Universe Next Door*, author Frank Swain defines the multiverse as:

"The multiverse is the hypothetical set of all universes. Together, these universes are thought to include everything that exists: time, space, matter, energy, and even the laws of physics that describe them."

These other universes go by many names: parallel universes, alternate realities, other worlds, child and parent universes, or simply "many worlds".

A common assumption in modern science is that if multiverses exist, they probably follow the same physical laws as ours. However, this might not necessarily be true. It's entirely possible that these universes follow completely different rules—rules that are unknown and unimaginable to us.

As we discussed earlier, science relies on *anumana pramana*—inference based on observation. Scientists require testable and observable evidence before accepting a claim as true. Yet, sometimes, truths exist that are beyond the scope of our current tools and technologies. History shows that many ideas once considered imaginary—like atoms or galaxies—were later proven true. Maybe the multiverse theory will follow a similar trajectory.

This brings us to the Vedic understanding of the universe and how it addresses this concept of the multiverse in a much more direct and detailed manner.

Multiverse in the Vedic Scriptures

The ancient Vedic texts of India, especially the *Puranas* and the Upanishads, speak in great detail about the creation of not just one universe, but many. Among these texts, the Srimad Bhagavatam (Bhagavata Purana) offers the most elaborate and spiritually rich descriptions of reality.

Unlike modern science, which relies on observation, the Vedic system accepts *shabda pramana*—truth that comes from divine sound or scripture. This means hearing from an authoritative source is, in itself, considered proof. In fact, Vedic knowledge is said to be *apaurusheya*, meaning it is not produced by any human but comes from the Supreme Divine source.

So, what does the Srimad Bhagavatam say about the multiverse?

Two Kinds of Creation

According to the Srimad Bhagavatam, there are two levels of creation:

1. Primary Creation – Done by Lord Maha-Vishnu, a form of the Supreme Lord.
2. Secondary Creation – Done by Lord Brahma, the first created being in each universe.

Before any creation happens, the Lord alone exists. In the *Aitareya Upanishad* (1.1.1–2), it is said:

"He (the Lord) glanced at the material energy... and He created all the worlds."

The Lord's glance is powerful and divine. It activates the material energy and brings universes into existence.

The Bhagavatam describes that when Maha-Vishnu exhales, countless universes emerge from the pores of His divine body. When He inhales, they are all drawn back in. While this may sound poetic or symbolic, it describes a spiritual reality. To give a relatable example, think of how beads of sweat form from the pores of our skin. In a similar way, entire universes are created and destroyed with Maha-Vishnu's breathing.

These universes float in a spiritual ocean called the Causal Ocean, and they can vary in size, structure, and complexity. Once a universe is formed, Lord Brahma is born within it and begins shaping and organizing it. He creates stars, planets, time, and different species of life. This process is called secondary creation.

The Meeting of Brahmas: Clear Proof of the Multiverse

There's a fascinating story in the Bhagavatam, as well as in the *Caitanya-caritamrita*, that directly speaks about the multiverse.

Once, when Lord Krishna was living in Dvaraka on Earth, Lord Brahma, the four-headed creator of our universe, came to meet Him. At the entrance, Krishna's gatekeeper asked Brahma a surprising question:

"Which Brahma are you?"

Brahma was confused. He thought he was the only Brahma. He replied,

"I am the four-headed Brahma, the father of the four Kumaras."

The gatekeeper went in and informed Krishna. Krishna smiled and invited Brahma inside. After greeting him, Krishna closed His eyes for a moment and entered a divine meditation.

Suddenly, countless other Brahmas from other universes appeared. Some had 10 heads, others had 100, some had 1,000, 10,000, a million, even hundreds of millions of heads! Each one came with their own Lord Shiva and King Indra. These beings were beyond anything the four-headed Brahma had ever imagined.

He realized that not only was his universe one among many, but that his own position was quite small compared to the other Brahmas who ruled far bigger and more complex universes.

This story clearly illustrates that Vedic literature accepts the multiverse not as a mere possibility, but as a fact. The Supreme Lord controls and maintains countless universes, each with its own creation process, elements, gods, and laws. And yet, the Supreme Lord remains one—beyond all of them.

Structure and Hierarchy in the Multiverse

From the scriptures, we learn that all universes are spherical and surrounded by coverings made of the five elements—earth, water, fire, air, and space. Each universe functions like a gigantic organization with many departments—creation, administration, air, water, food, life, and so on. These departments are managed by empowered beings (demigods), all working under the authority of the Supreme Lord.

Additionally, it is revealed that our universe—the one we inhabit—is one of the smallest, and our Brahma has just four heads. Other universes are far bigger and more complex. Their Brahmas have thousands or millions of heads, depending on the size and complexity of their creation.

Final Thoughts: What Can We Learn?

To conclude, the concept of a multiverse is not a fantasy or a recent invention; it has deep roots in ancient spiritual texts, particularly the Vedas. While contemporary science is beginning to explore this idea through theories and calculations, Vedic literature already provides vivid, detailed, and spiritually grounded explanations of multiple universes.

According to Vedic wisdom, the multiverse is not chaotic or random. Each universe is carefully created, maintained, and destroyed by divine will. Each has its own laws, time cycles, and destiny. However, all are ultimately under the control of the one Supreme Personality of Godhead—Sri Krishna.

As modern science continues to push the boundaries of knowledge, it may one day catch up with the truths already revealed in the Vedic scriptures. Until then, the concept of the multiverse remains a subject of fascination and a doorway to a deeper spiritual understanding of the grand design of creation.

CHAPTER 14

GOAL SETTING - SEEKING PERFECTION IN LIFE

A Life Without Goals – A Football Field Without Goalposts

Imagine a football field devoid of goalposts—22 players energetically running up and down, chasing the ball, but with no objective in sight. No matter how skilled or enthusiastic the players are, without a goal, the entire match becomes meaningless. That's what life is like when we do not set goals for ourselves. It's akin to boarding a train without knowing your destination. You might move rapidly and see many sights along the way, but without a clear direction, the journey itself becomes purposeless and disoriented.

Every being in existence must have some sort of goal. Goals give life direction, clarity, motivation, and focus. To live without goals is to live reactively, being tossed by circumstances rather than navigating life consciously. Only inert matter can exist without goals—stones, water, and air exist, but do not plan or strive. In contrast, sentient beings possess consciousness and intentionality. Even plants and animals, though lacking complex rationality, operate with basic instincts that drive them to survive, grow, reproduce, and protect themselves. These instincts serve as their automatic goals for existence.

Human beings, endowed with the gift of higher intelligence and consciousness, are uniquely positioned to define and pursue elevated goals—not just for survival but for purpose, fulfillment, and transcendence. As we mature, we naturally begin to contemplate life beyond basic needs. We start to ask ourselves: What do I want from life? Why am I here? What's the purpose of my talents, my relationships, my suffering, and my joy?

Maslow's Hierarchy and Human Motivation

In the 20th century, psychologist Abraham Maslow proposed a now-famous model called Maslow's Hierarchy of Needs, which attempts to explain human motivation. This framework is often depicted as a pyramid with five levels, moving from the most fundamental physical needs to the highest spiritual aspirations:

1. Physiological Needs – Food, water, warmth, rest.
2. Safety Needs – Security, stability, protection.
3. Love and Belonging – Relationships, friendships, emotional connection.
4. Esteem Needs – Respect, accomplishment, recognition.
5. Self-Actualization – The desire to become the best version of oneself.

Maslow believed that lower-level needs must be reasonably satisfied before a person can fully devote themselves to higher-level goals. For instance, a hungry person is unlikely to be interested in abstract ideas of meaning or philosophy until their hunger is addressed. Yet in real life, this progression is not always linear. Some people may strive for artistic excellence while living in poverty, while others may pursue spiritual enlightenment despite lacking emotional connections. The pursuit of goals is often simultaneous and overlapping, driven by a mix of internal and external pressures.

But beyond these, what lies at the pinnacle of human aspiration?

The Vedic Vision: The Four *Purusharthas*

While Maslow outlined a psychological model, the ancient Vedic literature of India presents a spiritual and moral framework known as the *Purusharthas*, or the four goals of human life. The term "Purushartha" is a compound of "Purusha" (person or soul) and "Artha" (goal or meaning). These four goals are:

1. *Dharma* – Righteousness, moral duty, spiritual values.
2. *Artha* – Economic development, material prosperity.
3. *Kama* – Fulfillment of desires, emotional satisfaction.
4. *Moksha* – Liberation, spiritual freedom, transcendence.

These goals are not isolated compartments, but rather a progressive ladder. Each goal builds upon the previous one, guiding a person from survival and enjoyment to responsibility and ultimately to transcendence.

Let's explore each of them in greater depth.

Dharma – The Foundation of Human Life

The first and most essential goal is *Dharma*. Dharma does not merely refer to "religion" in the narrow sense; it encompasses ethical living, duties, responsibilities, and alignment with cosmic order. It represents the universal law that sustains and upholds society, much like gravity sustains the physical universe.

In the modern world, many attempt to pursue wealth (*Artha*) and pleasure (*Kama*) without first grounding themselves in *Dharma*. This is akin to building a skyscraper without a solid foundation—it's bound to collapse. Without *Dharma*, there is no inner compass, no discipline, and no sense of responsibility or boundaries. Society descends into a chaotic race for personal gain, leading to stress, crime, exploitation, and environmental degradation.

Animals act based on instinct and don't need moral guidelines. However, humans, endowed with free will and higher reasoning must voluntarily adopt principles to live harmoniously. *Dharma* provides the framework that distinguishes human life from animal existence.

Artha – The Pursuit of Prosperity

Once grounded in *Dharma*, a person can responsibly pursue *Artha*, or economic prosperity. *Artha* is essential because one needs resources for survival, family, social contribution, and personal growth. However, when *Artha* is pursued without *Dharma*, it becomes greed and leads to exploitation, corruption, and unprincipled behaviour.

In today's world, we see a frantic chase for money, often at the cost of fundamental values. Many people are willing to compromise honesty, integrity, and compassion just to accumulate more wealth. This path leads to various forms of bondage—legal, emotional, and karmic. The Vedic system trains individuals from an early age to view wealth not as an end in itself, but as a tool to serve a higher purpose.

The Bhagavad Gita describes wealth as a double-edged sword. If acquired and used properly, it can uplift society and free individuals for deeper pursuits. However, if misused, it can entrap the soul in endless cycles of desire and frustration.

Kama – Enjoyment in Moderation

Having earned wealth honestly, a person may then seek *Kama*—pleasure, fulfillment, and emotional and sensual satisfaction. The Vedic tradition doesn't deny or condemn enjoyment; rather, it teaches how to enjoy responsibly, without causing harm to self or others. It advocates balanced enjoyment guided by *Dharma*, not indulgence driven by impulse.

True enjoyment comes not from excess, but from harmony. For instance, eating sweets when you have diabetes may bring momentary pleasure, but it leads to long-term suffering. Similarly, enjoyment that violates natural laws and moral duties results in karmic bondage.

Real happiness lies in sustainable enjoyment—pleasure that uplifts, not degrades. The Vedas refer to this as "regulated sense enjoyment"—enjoy, but within boundaries. This ensures that happiness today does not turn into suffering tomorrow.

Moksha – The Quest for Liberation

The first three goals—*Dharma, Artha*, and *Kama*—are largely oriented toward this life and, to some extent, future lives. However, the fourth goal, *Moksha*, is of a different order altogether. *Moksha* signifies liberation from the cycle of birth and death, freeing us from the suffering and limitations of material existence. It is the realization of one's eternal identity beyond the body and mind.

Why seek *Moksha*? Because no matter how refined our material pursuits are, they cannot provide complete, permanent satisfaction. Every material pleasure is temporary and comes mixed with suffering—separation, change, loss, or dependence. The soul, being eternal and spiritual, can never be permanently satisfied with temporary and material things. *Moksha* is the soul's homecoming.

Beyond *Moksha* – *Prema Pumartho Mahan*

While *Moksha* may seem like the ultimate goal, the Vedic scriptures, particularly the Bhagavata Purana and the teachings of Lord Chaitanya Mahaprabhu—an incarnation of Lord Krishna, who appeared in Nadia, West Bengal (India) in the 15th century AD—speak of an even higher goal - *Prema*, or loving devotional service to the Supreme Lord. Sri Chaitanya declared: "*Prema Pumartho Mahan*", which means "Love (*Prema)* for God is the greatest of all goals."

Why is *Prema* higher than *Moksha*? This is so because *Moksha* represents freedom from suffering, while *Prema* signifies unlimited joy. *Moksha* offers peace; *Prema* provides ecstasy of the highest order. In *Prema*, the soul is liberated from bondage and is actively engaged in a loving relationship with the Divine. This relationship brings the highest form of satisfaction because it reconnects the soul to its original nature and source—God.

The Two Universal Goals of All Beings

Ultimately, all living beings—consciously or unconsciously—seek two things in everything they do:

1. Happiness
2. Freedom from problems

Every decision, pursuit, and dream can be traced back to these two driving forces. However, unless one connects to the spiritual reality through *Moksha* and *Bhakti,* one cannot attain these goals in their pure form. Material happiness is temporary and plagued by challenges. Only spiritual happiness is permanent and pure.

The Prison Analogy

Life in the material world is often compared to life in a prison. Although one may find temporary comforts in prison—such as timely food or a space to live—the ultimate goal remains freedom. Similarly, our life here, no matter how successful externally, is a limited and temporary reality. True freedom lies in returning to the spiritual world, our real home.

Conclusion: Set Your Goals Wisely

Just as a football match without goals is meaningless, a life without purposeful goals is wasted. While short-term goals like career success, relationships, and health are important, they must be aligned with long-term and ultimate goals. Without spiritual vision, even success can become a form of failure. However, when one aligns every thought, word, and action toward attaining pure love for God, everything else falls into place. Such a life is not only meaningful, but also eternally blissful.

Let us, therefore, set our sights on the highest goal—*Prema*, the loving service of God—and live with clarity, conviction, and purpose.

CHAPTER 15

YOGA - THE SACRED CONNECTION

What is Yoga?

The word "Yoga" is perhaps one of the most well-known words with Indian origins, recognized worldwide. Similar words include "Karma", "Guru", "Avatar", etc. Interestingly, most of these words carry spiritual connotations. India has long been a destination for spiritual seekers from around the globe. Even the West looks to the East for spiritual enlightenment. This is not surprising given India's rich Vedic culture, a vast treasure trove of spiritual knowledge. However, the meaning of the word "yoga" has become so diversified and diluted that its true significance has unfortunately been lost to a major section of the world. Few people truly grasp the profound spiritual essence of this word.

As the title of this chapter suggests, the etymology of the word "yoga" stems from the Sanskrit root word *"yuj"*, which means to join or connect. This is also where the English word "yoke" derives from—the piece of wood that binds two oxen together. The words join, connect, or yoke suggest a union between two entities. The Bhagavad Gita and many other Vedic scriptures explain that Yoga represents the most sacred connection between the Soul and God, as well as between ourselves and God.

Different Meanings of the Word "Yoga"

The term "Yoga" encompasses several connotations, including *pranayama, asanas*, a *sattvic* lifestyle, exercise, etc. There are also numerous variations when prefixes and suffixes are added, leading to types of Yoga. While some of these interpretations may be valid, they often obscure the true meaning of the word. Hence, there is a need to discuss the actual meaning of the word "Yoga", which is "Sacred Connection". Understanding this is crucial because without grasping the actual meaning, one may only experience limited physical and mental benefits from practices like breathing exercises and poses, missing the immense spiritual advantages. In fact, one may overlook the ultimate benefit of life that Yoga offers: the revival of the sacred connection between ourselves and God.

Yoga - The Connection between Us and God

Each soul, each one of us, possesses an individual, eternal, unique connection with God—a relationship between two persons, us and the Supreme Person, God. In the Bhagavad Gita, Lord Krishna states in Chapter 15, Verse 7, that the innumerable souls are His part and parcels. The words used in this connection are "*Mamaiva amsa*" and "*Sanatana*", which translate to "My eternal fragmented part and parcels". This also means that the connection between us and God can never be broken. A crude analogy is that blood relationships in a family remain even if they are strained. However, strained relationships need to be revived and rejuvenated. Therefore, Yoga acts as both a noun and a verb—something that must be practised to revive this sacred connection between us and God. Given the depth of this topic, I plan to write a separate book on it later. Here, I will present some key aspects.

Benefits of Yoga - A Sacred Connection

Why is it vital to revive our relationship with God through this "Sacred Connection"? What benefits arise from it? How can we connect with God easily in this busy modern age? These are crucial questions which we will explore now.

One fundamental truth is that parts have value only when connected to the whole. For example, a small screw is valuable when it is part of a machine; separated from it, it is useless. Similarly, a mobile phone is only useful when it can connect to electricity to charge. A tap has no value if it is not connected to the water pipeline. In the same vein, the Vedic scriptures emphasize that the soul holds no value unless it revives its relationship with the Supreme Lord. Many of the challenges faced by living beings stem from this disconnect with God. The *Ishopanishad,* regarded as the best of all Upanishads, states that all feelings of incompleteness arise from not being properly connected to the Supreme Whole—God. By forging this connection, we can mitigate both our short- and long-term problems.

An example frequently cited by Srila Prabhupada, the Founder Guru of ISKCON worldwide, involves the numerical digits 1 and 0. He explained that if you take the number 10 and place zeros to the left of 1, its value doesn't increase. However, if you add zeros to the right of 1, the value increases. The idea is that the 1 must come first; if zeros accompany the 1, their value increases because the 1 gives them worth. If the 1 is shifted to the right, its value diminishes, and without the 1, even a million zeros amount to nothing.

What can we learn from this? Srila Prabhupada stated that the 1 represents God, and the zeros symbolize all other goals in our lives. If we establish a solid connection with God and prioritize Him, all other aspirations in our lives gain value. Conversely, the more we distance ourselves from God, the less value our lives hold, even if we possess everything else for our comfort.

From Miniscule To Mighty - Achieving the Impossible Through Yoga

Another example from the scriptures is the story of the famous king, Dhruva. As a five-year-old child, Dhruva faced deep humiliation when he sought affection from his father, the king of the whole world in ancient times. This fuelled his determination to find solace. At such a tender age, instead of playing like other children, he accepted Narada Muni as his guru and embarked into the forest to perform penances and please God through Bhakti Yoga. Remarkably, within six months, Dhruva succeeded in his austerities and achieved the impossible. Lord Vishnu appeared before him, granting him several blessings.

How did a mere child, insulted by his father, transform into such a powerful figure? The answer remains consistent: when you connect with God, the most powerful entity, you can achieve the seemingly impossible.

Four Benefits of Connecting with God

In the last verse of the Bhagavad Gita, Sanjaya, the advisor to king Dhritarashtra, reveals four benefits of connecting with the Supreme Lord. According to him, through connection with God, we receive *Sri* (or Lakshmi, representing wealth), *Vijaya* (victory in life's struggles), *Bhuti* (extraordinary power), and *Niti* (morality).

A simple example is of a cyclist who connects with a moving tractor trolley and gains the speed and power of the vehicle. In the Kurukshetra war, the Pandavas, despite having fewer fighters and resources, triumphed over the Kauravas, who had the resources of the whole world at their command and several other undefeatable warriors on their side. What is the reason for this?

The Pandavas had the support of Lord Krishna, who, although having vowed not to lift a weapon in the war, provided divine guidance that led the Pandavas to victory.

What other lessons can be learnt from this? No matter how powerful one may be in this world, without a connection with God, their future is bleak. Conversely, regardless of our current situation, if we turn to God, our greatest weaknesses can be transformed into our strongest assets by Him.

How Our Greatest Weaknesses Can Become Our Greatest Strengths through Sacred Connection

This idea is encapsulated in the following inspirational story:

A young boy who was born without a left arm was sent to judo lessons by his mother to help boost his confidence. He began training with an old Japanese master.

During every practice session, the master taught the boy only one throw—a single technique he repeated over and over.

Frequently, the one-armed boy would see other students learning different techniques and question the master about why he wasn't learning anything else.

The master always replied, "Just focus on this one throw. Keep practising."

Several months later, at the state judo championships, the master entered the young boy.

The young boy was terrified.

The first match began, and to the astonishment of all the spectators, the one-armed boy grabbed his opponent and effortlessly flipped him to the ground, winning instantly!

The second round proved slightly more challenging, but the boy again executed his sole technique and emerged victorious.

The same scenario unfolded in the third and fourth rounds, leading the boy to the tournament final against a much larger, stronger, and more experienced opponent, who had won the tournament for three consecutive years.

It seemed the young boy was outmatched. The referee and the organizers of the tournament approached the master, asking if he wanted to withdraw his student.

"No," said the master. "We will fight."

As the final match began, the entire crowd was on the edge of their seats. The opponent stepped forward, grabbed the young one-armed boy, and pulled him closer. For a moment, it seemed as if it was all over...

But then, the one-armed boy reached out with his right hand, stepped in, and BOOM – he threw his opponent flat on his back, winning the match!

The crowd went wild – the one-armed boy was now the state Judo Champion!

On the drive home, the young boy asked his teacher, "Was this a set-up? Did they just let me win because I have only one arm? I only know one technique, while these fellows know hundreds!"

The teacher replied, "No, you won fair and square. There are two reasons for your success. First, you mastered one of the most devastating techniques in judo. Second, the only known way to defend against that throw is to grab the left arm, which you do not have.

What was seen as a big weakness became his greatest strength. When we connect with God, a similar transformation occurs. Yoga, therefore, serves as the connection that revives our true potential—the potential of the soul.

Let's connect with God today and make our lives successful!

CHAPTER 16

THE YOGA LADDER

Introducing the Yoga Ladder

In the previous chapter, we discussed how "Yoga" is the sacred, eternal connection between the soul (*atma*) and the Supreme Lord (*Paramatma*). Although this connection is never truly broken, in our conditioned state, it often remains dormant, like a fire covered by ashes or a seed lying deep in dry soil. Through spiritual practice, this connection can be revived and fully awakened. When it is, the result is nothing less than the ultimate perfection of life—pure love for God. This love is not just a fleeting emotional experience, but the soul's original nature, an unending and ever-deepening bond of devotion and joy.

Importantly, true love can only be experienced between persons. One cannot love an impersonal energy or a formless idea. Just as one person loves another—through relationships, emotions, and service—the soul can only truly love God when God is approached as a person. And He is the Supreme Person, full of beauty, charm, sweetness, compassion, and all opulences.

Unlimited happiness, beyond the reach of material senses, awaits those who complete the process of Yoga and fully reconnect with this Divine Person. While other benefits of Yoga—like good physical health, peace of mind, emotional stability, moral conduct, and a disciplined life—are certainly helpful and attractive, they are actually secondary or fringe benefits. The real treasure lies in the revival of our eternal, loving relationship with God, which alone satisfies the deepest longing of the heart.

To understand this connection better, we can compare it to how we connect to the internet. Some connections are slow, some are faster, and others, like broadband or Wi-Fi, are blazing fast. Similarly, there are different methods or approaches to connect with the Supreme Lord, each with its own speed and depth. In the *Bhagavad Gita As It Is*, Srila Prabhupada explains that these approaches form a Yoga Ladder—a gradual and elevating system that brings the soul closer to God step by step.

This Yoga Ladder consists of four primary rungs—Karma Yoga, Jnana Yoga, Astanga Yoga, and finally, Bhakti Yoga. Just as a staircase has many steps but leads to a single destination, the various yogas are meant to guide the soul toward the supreme goal of *Bhakti*, or loving devotion to God. Let us now explore each of these steps one by one.

Karma Yoga – The Yoga of Action

Karma Yoga is the foundational rung on the Yoga ladder. The word "karma" means action—physical, verbal, and mental—and "yoga" means connection. Therefore, Karma Yoga refers to connecting with the Lord through one's daily work and responsibilities, using mediums like the mind, words and the body.

In this system, a person performs only those actions that are prescribed in the Vedic scriptures, avoiding prohibited or sinful actions. The focus is on selfless service, doing one's duties not for personal enjoyment, but with the aim to please the Supreme Lord. Instead of living just to enjoy the weekends or indulge in sense gratification, the Karma Yogi leads a responsible household life with God at the centre of all activities.

Each person has a unique combination of body and mind, known as their psychophysical nature. Based on this nature, the Vedic system called *Varnashramadharma* prescribes appropriate duties that align with one's nature. When one performs these duties with detachment and spiritual consciousness, that work becomes Yoga.

A Karma Yogi is not just a moral or hardworking person. They study scriptures like the Bhagavad Gita and Srimad Bhagavatam, gaining an understanding of the deeper purpose of life. This spiritual knowledge leads to detachment—not indifference, but freedom from selfish motives. Gradually, the Karma Yogi becomes purified and begins to see that even the highest material goals—wealth, fame, and enjoyment—are temporary and limited. They seek liberation from the cycle of birth and death. As this detachment deepens, they naturally become inclined to study and contemplate more, thus entering the next rung of the ladder—Jnana Yoga.

Jnana Yoga – The Yoga of Knowledge

Jnana Yoga is the second step on the Yoga Ladder. "Jnana" means knowledge, particularly the knowledge that distinguishes spirit from matter, truth from illusion, and the eternal from the temporary.

Jnana Yoga focuses on connecting with God through spiritual wisdom. A Jnana Yogi usually adopts a life of renunciation, surrendering not only sense gratification but also household responsibilities, wealth, and material attachments. The Jnana Yogi studies the Upanishads, the Vedanta Sutras, and other Vedantic texts, often withdrawing from society to focus on understanding the soul (*atma*) and the impersonal spiritual energy (*Brahman*).

The ultimate goal of the Jnana Yogi is liberation (*moksha*)—freedom from the repeated cycle of birth and death. They meditate on the impersonal *Brahman*, the formless aspect of God. Their philosophy posits that the soul and God are ultimately one, and liberation means merging into that oneness.

However, even this elevated goal is not the complete truth. The Bhagavad Gita explains that the impersonal *Brahman* is simply the effulgence, or glowing aura, emanating from the personal form of the Supreme Lord. If a Jnana Yogi is fortunate, humble, and comes in contact with a Bhakti Yogi, they may be inspired to rise to a higher level of realization by taking up Bhakti Yoga.

Astanga Yoga – The Yoga of Meditation

Astanga Yoga, sometimes referred to as Raja Yoga or Hatha Yoga, is the third stage on the Yoga Ladder. The word "Astanga" means "eight limbs", which are:

1. *Yama* – Moral restraints (e.g., truthfulness, non-violence)
2. *Niyama* – Positive disciplines (e.g., cleanliness, self-control)
3. *Asana* – Physical postures that support meditation
4. *Pranayama* – Regulation of breath to control the mind
5. *Pratyahara* – Withdrawal of the senses from sense objects
6. *Dharana* – One-pointed concentration on the Supersoul
7. *Dhyana* – Deep meditation on the Supersoul
8. *Samadhi* – Complete absorption in the object of meditation

In Astanga Yoga, meditation (*Dhyana*) is the core practice. The goal is to concentrate on the Supersoul (*Paramatma*) in the heart. The Bhagavad Gita and Srimad Bhagavatam explain that this *Paramatma* manifests as a four-armed divine form of the Lord, who witnesses all our actions and resides within every living being.

However, due to the influence of impersonal philosophies, many Astanga Yogis aim not to serve this Supersoul, but to dissolve their own identity and merge into the impersonal *Brahman*. Despite having glimpsed the personal aspect of God, they remain attached to the impersonal conception. Unless such yogis receive the association of a Bhakti Yogi, they rarely progress beyond this stage.

Bhakti Yoga – The Yoga of Love

Bhakti Yoga is the final and highest rung on the Yoga Ladder. The word "Bhakti" means devotion, love, and affectionate service offered to the Supreme Lord. While other forms of yogas require detachment, renunciation, or complex meditation, Bhakti Yoga is fundamentally about loving God with heart and soul.

A Bhakti Yogi views God not as an abstract force or a distant energy, but as the Supreme Person—Krishna, who embodies all divine qualities and relationships. Just as we naturally feel affection for our loved ones, the soul in its pure state feels spontaneous and intense love for Krishna. This love is eternal, and Bhakti Yoga serves to reawaken it.

Bhakti Yoga is unique in that it can be practised by anyone, regardless of age, background, qualification, or lifestyle. It is not limited to monks or scholars; a student, a housewife, a businessman, or a child—anyone can engage in *Bhakti* through simple but powerful practices such as:

- Chanting the Holy Names of the Lord (especially the *Hare Krishna Mahamantra*)
- Hearing about Krishna's pastimes from scriptures like the Srimad Bhagavatam
- Worshipping the Deity form of the Lord
- Serving devotees and the mission of Krishna
- Offering food, time, energy, etc.

The most beautiful aspect of Bhakti Yoga is that it's not a one-sided effort. As we take even small steps toward Krishna with love, He personally reciprocates, guiding and helping us. The Lord is conquered only by love, and He eagerly waits to embrace the soul that sincerely desires to serve Him.

Conclusion

Thus, the Yoga Ladder illustrates a progressive journey toward God—from Karma Yoga (action) to Jnana Yoga (knowledge), then to Astanga Yoga (meditation), and finally to Bhakti Yoga (love and devotion). While each of these paths offers valuable insights and practices, they are only complete when they culminate in *Bhakti*, which represents the natural and eternal occupation of the soul.

Bhakti Yoga is the only process that fully satisfies the Supreme Lord and guides the soul back to its original home—the spiritual world, a realm of eternal service, joy, and loving relationships. It is not a slow ascent, but a divine elevator, swiftly lifting the sincere practitioner to the highest perfection.

Remarkably, one does not need to progress step by step through each stage. From any rung—whether Karma, Jnana, or Astanga Yoga—one can directly pursue Bhakti Yoga. This direct path is made possible through association with a Bhakti Yogi, a pure devotee whose heart is filled with love for God. Just as fire ignites dry wood, the presence of such a devotee awakens dormant love in others.

In this dark age of Kali Yuga, where distractions, anxieties, and conflicts are pervasive, Bhakti Yoga shines as a beacon of hope. It is the simplest, sweetest, and most powerful path, inviting us all to return to our eternal home, where love reigns supreme, and the soul dances in divine joy.

CHAPTER 17

GURU - THE TRANSPARENT VIA MEDIA TO CONNECT WITH GOD

What is the Meaning of "Guru"?

The term "Guru" is a Sanskrit word, which literally means "heavy" or "grave/serious". It also refers to a spiritual leader or an expert teacher in any field. Here, we limit its meaning to a spiritual leader. A spiritual leader is "grave" because they understand the essential truths of life and aspire to guide others toward these truths. Like the term "yoga", which encompasses various meanings, "Guru" can also signify many things. There are countless interpretations of spirituality and, consequently, innumerable types of Gurus in the world. However, having explored the essence of spirituality in the last chapter, we should now focus on understanding the essence of a "Guru" or spiritual leader. We need to discern the qualities, eligibility, and lifestyle of a genuine spiritual teacher to avoid being misled in our quest for the absolute truth.

Why Have a Middleman Between Myself and God?

Some people claim that since they have encountered numerous fraudulent Gurus or have heard about them, they prefer to avoid them altogether. They view Gurus as unnecessary middlemen who stand between them and God, believing it is best to approach

God directly. However, this response often stems from a knee-jerk reaction to a problem. When an eye causes issues, we do not remove the eye; instead, we remove the problem by consulting an ophthalmologist. Even if we have experienced deceitful doctors in the past, we do not abandon seeking medical help and start treating ourselves. We just have to be careful when selecting our doctors. Similarly, while there are counterfeit goods in the market, including fake currency, we do not stop using currency or goods altogether; rather, we learn to differentiate between fake and real. The same concept applies to Gurus, who are essentially spiritual doctors.

Our next question is how to distinguish between genuine and fake Gurus. For this, we need to understand the qualifications of each.

Qualifications of a Genuine Guru

So, who is a genuine spiritual Guru? To understand this, let's refer to a few verses from Vedic scriptures that can clarify our understanding:

1. *"tad vijnanartham sa gurum evabhigacchet samit panih srotriyam brahma-nistham" - Mundaka Upanishad, 1.2.12*

Translation: "To learn the transcendental subject matter, one must approach a spiritual master. In doing so, he should carry fuel to burn in sacrifice. The symptom of such a spiritual master is that he is an expert in understanding the Vedic conclusion, and therefore, he constantly engages in the service of the Supreme Personality of Godhead."

2. *"tasmad gurum prapadyeta jijñasuh sreya uttamam*
   sabde pare ca nisnatam brahmany upasamasrayam" -
   Srimad-Bhagavatam, 11.3.21

Translation: "Therefore any person who seriously desires real happiness must seek a bona fide spiritual master and take shelter of him by initiation. The qualification of the bona fide guru is that he has realized the conclusions of the scriptures by deliberation and is able to convince others of these conclusions. Such great personalities, who have taken shelter of the Supreme Godhead, leaving aside all material considerations, should be understood to be bona fide spiritual masters."

3. *"vaco vegam manasah krodha-vegam jihvavegam udaropastha-vegam etan vegan yo visaheta dhirah sarvam apimam prithivim sa shishyat"*

Translation: "A sober person who can tolerate the urge to speak, the mind's demands, the actions of anger and the urges of the tongue, belly and genitals is qualified to make disciples all over the world."

More about a Genuine Guru:

The majority of people approach a Guru seeking blessings and miracles, often for the fulfillment of material desires or the resolution of personal problems. However, the Vedic scriptures state that these motivations are not the proper reasons for approaching a Guru. There are numerous experts available for these matters. A Guru should be approached solely for the purpose of attaining spiritual perfection. Only those who are serious about understanding the deeper secrets of life, our relationship with God, and how we can permanently end our suffering should seek a Guru.

Qualifications of a Genuine Spiritual Guru

1. The hallmark of a true Guru is that they have not created their own teachings, but have received spiritual knowledge from the correct sources. These include the four Vaishnava Sampradayas or an unbroken chain of disciplic succession that traces back to God Himself. Not only must the Guru have learned from the right sources, but they must also have

applied this knowledge in their own life and be spiritually situated. A genuine Guru thoroughly understands the conclusions of the Vedic scriptures and possesses the ability to impart the same and satisfactorily address the questions of seekers.

2. A true spiritual Guru never claims to be God. Instead, the Guru serves as a perfect lens, helping seekers gain clarity. There is a prayer that reflects this idea: "*Om ajnana timirandhasya jnananjana salakaya, caksur unmilitam yena tasmai sri gurave namah*", which means, "I offer my respectful obeisances unto my spiritual master, who has opened my eyes, which were blinded by the darkness of ignorance, with the torchlight of knowledge." A Guru, therefore, is someone who helps seekers to attain God and acts as a servant of the Supreme Lord, teaching love and service toward God.
3. An authentic spiritual Guru is known as an *Acharya,* which in Sanskrit means "a teacher who teaches by his or her own example". The word "*acharya*" stems from the word "*aachar*" or one's behaviour. Unlike many pseudo-teachers who lead double lives, presenting one facade publicly while acting differently in private, a true Guru remains consistent. They live in accordance with their teachings, embodying integrity and setting a proper example for others.
4. A genuine Guru possesses the ability to manage the demands of the mind, words, senses, and body, including the genitals. Rather than indulging freely in sensory pleasures, a true Guru makes a conscious effort to restrain the senses and channel them into the service of God. Throughout history, there have been false Gurus who engage in sinful activities

in the name of spirituality and religion while claiming to transcend all reproach and correction.

5. A genuine Guru is a pure devotee of the Lord, deeply immersed in activities related to Him. Their days and nights are filled with spiritual activities, prayer, and meditation. Even their professional work is approached as an offering to the Supreme Lord; their entire life is an offering to the Lord.
6. The teachings of a bonafide Guru are grounded in Vedic scriptures, especially conclusive texts such as the Bhagavad Gita and Srimad Bhagavatam. An illustrative example could be that of professors in a university who base their lectures on the textbooks provided or sanctioned by the institution. If a professor teaches something that diverges from the textbook, a red flag is raised. If their teachings significantly differ from those of other respected figures in the field, or if they dismiss the works of eminent personalities, skepticism should arise.

Just as we are cautious when making significant decisions—such as purchasing items, choosing careers, or selecting a life partner—we should also exercise caution on the spiritual path when choosing a Guru. The aforementioned points can serve as guidance in this regard. Once we find a genuine Guru, it is crucial to fully submit and surrender to their teachings, integrating these lessons into our lives to ensure success on our spiritual journey.

Can we search for a Guru? Certainly. One must pray to the Supreme Lord for guidance and seek a genuine Guru who exhibits the characteristics outlined above and more.

Happy Seeking!

CHAPTER 18

DHARMA - THE INHERENT CHARACTERISTIC OF LIFE

What is *Dharma*?

The Sanskrit word "*Dharma*" is said to have no equivalent translation in English or any other language. Many languages have words without direct counterparts. However, we will attempt to explore the meaning of *Dharma*. This term appears repeatedly throughout almost all the Vedic scriptures, including the Bhagavad Gita and the Srimad Bhagvatam. *Dharma* carries several connotations, including spirituality, duty, occupation, righteousness, morality, laws, and the "right way of living". Thus, this concept is significant throughout life, from beginning to end. Let's examine some of the different aspects of *Dharma*.

Dharma is the first of the four *purusharthas* or stages of life, the other three being *Artha, Kama*, and *Moksha* in that order. This sequence emphasizes that before pursuing *Artha* (wealth) and *Kama* (enjoyment), one must first learn to be morally accountable and spiritual. Following this order leads to detachment and the pursuit of *Moksha* (liberation) at the end of life. Unfortunately, many today focus solely on *Artha* and *Kama*, seeking to earn money by any means and enjoy life with little restraint. This approach often leads to chaos, heavy karmic repercussions, and suffering, which carry over into future lives.

In earlier times, Gurukuls (traditional schools) provided training in all four *Purusharthas,* with an emphasis on following *Dharma*. To embrace *Dharma* means to accept the authority of the Vedas and lead a life aligned with the laws and guidelines they outline. Essentially, one acknowledges God as the Supreme authority in their life, dedicating thoughts, words, and actions to the Supreme Lord as per the teachings of the Vedas, particularly the Bhagavad Gita and Srimad Bhagavatam. The Supreme Lord being the topmost authority, individuals are assured of "right" direction in the many crossroads of life and the various temptations it presents.

The Vedas contain primarily three sections or stages of *Dharma,* and progress is made by following these stages gradually. These stages are known as *Karma-kanda*, *Jnana-kanda*, and *Bhakti-kanda*.

1. *Karma-kanda* – *Dharma* through Duties and Rituals

At the initial level, the Vedas prescribe *Karma-kanda*, which involves rituals, duties, and prescribed actions aimed at material progress and pious living. This includes *yajnas* (sacrifices), *vratas* (vows), charity, and proper conduct according to one's social and spiritual position. The purpose of *Karma-kanda* is to gradually purify the individual by encouraging good habits, responsibility, and discipline. However, if one remains attached to mere rituals without higher understanding, they risk becoming trapped in material desires rather than advancing toward spiritual realization.

2. *Jnana-kanda* – *Dharma* through Knowledge and Renunciation

As one matures, they enter *Jnana-kanda*, where the focus shifts from external rituals to philosophical contemplation, knowledge, and detachment from material life. This stage is marked by enquiry into the nature of the self (*atman*), the impermanence of the world, and the need for spiritual liberation. The Upanishads emphasize this level, urging one to seek *Brahman* (the Absolute Truth) beyond transient pleasures and pains. However, mere knowledge is not enough; one must go beyond intellectual speculation to experience true realization.

3. *Bhakti-kanda* – *Dharma* through Devotion and Loving Service

The highest stage of *dharma* is *Bhakti-kanda*, where one engages in pure devotional service (Bhakti Yoga) to the Supreme Lord. This stage transcends mere duty and philosophical speculation, leading to a state where all actions are performed as offerings to the Lord with love and devotion. The Bhagavad Gita (18.66) concludes on this note, with Lord Krishna saying:

"*Sarva-dharman parityajya mam ekam sharanam vraja*"
Translation: "Abandon all varieties of dharma and simply surrender unto Me."

Here, Lord Krishna teaches that the highest form of *dharma* is surrendering to Him in love, beyond ritualistic duties and mere intellectual knowledge. This path leads to true liberation (*moksha*) and eternal bliss.

Dharma and the *Varnashrama* System

Another interpretation of the word "*dharma*" relates to occupational duties. To maintain harmony in society, the Vedas organize *dharma* into the *varna* (social) and *ashrama* (life stages) systems, collectively known as "*Varnashrama Dharma*".

1. The Four *Varnas* (Occupational Duties)

Dharma varies for different individuals based on their nature (*guna*) and work (*karma*). The Bhagavad Gita (4.13) explains:

"Chatur-varnyam maya srishtam guna-karma-vibhagashah"
Translation: "The four varnas were created by Me, based on qualities and work."

- Brahmanas (intellectuals and priests) – Their *dharma* is to cultivate wisdom, teach scriptures, and guide society in spiritual values.
- Kshatriyas (warriors and leaders) – Their *dharma* is to protect and govern the other three *varnas*, as well as the vulnerable members of society, such as cows, the elderly, women, and children, in a righteous manner.
- Vaishyas (merchants and farmers) – Their *dharma* is to protect cows by caring for them in *goshalas*, and to manage commerce, trade, and agriculture.
- Shudras (labourers and artisans) – Their *dharma* is to assist society by providing skilled labour to the other three classes.

Each *varna* has unique duties, and when these duties are followed sincerely, it leads to both material harmony and spiritual progress.

2. The Four *Ashramas* (Stages of Life)

Just as society is divided into four *varnas*, an individual's life is also divided into four *ashramas*, each with its own *dharma:*

- Brahmacharya (student life) – This stage focuses on discipline, learning, and celibacy under a guru, covering the first 25 years of life.
- Grihastha (householder life) – This stage involves responsibilities related to marriage, family, and earning a living righteously, typically from ages 25 to 50 .
- Vanaprastha (retired life) – This stage involves gradual detachment from material affairs and focus on spiritual life, spanning the ages of 50 to 75.
- Sannyasa (renounced life) – This final stage entails complete renunciation and dedicating oneself fully to God, from the age of 75 onwards.

By following this system, one can progress step by step toward the ultimate goal, i.e. loving service to the Supreme Lord.

Adharma – The Opposite of *Dharma*

When one strays from *dharma*, it leads to *adharma* (irreligion or unrighteousness). *Adharma* manifests as selfishness, dishonesty, cruelty, material greed, and disregard for spiritual values. The Bhagavad Gita (16.7) describes how those engaged in *adharma* do not understand what is right and what is wrong.

In modern times, many people have neglected *dharma*, leading to corruption, crime, environmental destruction, and spiritual ignorance. However, by reviving *dharma* in both personal and collective lives, society can attain peace, happiness, and spiritual fulfillment.

The Universal Nature of *Dharma*

Though *dharma* is often associated with Hinduism, its principles are universal. Every religion teaches moral values, honesty, compassion, and devotion to God. The essence of *dharma* is not limited to rituals or sectarian identities, but includes truthfulness, kindness, and spiritual realization.

A famous verse from the Mahabharata (Shanti Parva 109.10) summarizes this concept:

"*Dharma eva hato hanti, dharmo rakshati rakshitah*"
Translation: "One who destroys Dharma is destroyed by Dharma; one who protects Dharma is protected by Dharma."

This means that living in accordance with *dharma* ensures protection and prosperity, while neglecting it leads to downfall.

Dharma in the Modern World

In today's fast-paced, technology-driven world, how can one practice *dharma*? Here are some practical suggestions:

1. Live a life of integrity – Be honest, responsible, and fair in all your dealings.
2. Respect all living beings – Follow *ahimsa* (non-violence) and care for nature.
3. Balance material and spiritual life – Earn ethically, but do not neglect your spiritual growth.
4. Practise *Bhakti* – Chant the *Hare Krishna mantra*, read scriptures, and serve others.
5. Seek knowledge – Understand the purpose of life beyond temporary material achievements.

By incorporating these principles, one can lead a life of purpose and fulfillment.

Conclusion – The Pinnacle of *Dharma*

Dharma is not just a set of rules, but the very foundation of human life. It ensures that individuals and society progress in harmony with divine principles. The ultimate *dharma* of all living beings is to serve and love God, as stated in the Srimad Bhagavatam (1.2.6):

"*Sa vai pumsam paro dharmo yato bhaktir adhokshaje*"
Translation: "The highest Dharma is that which leads to pure devotion to the Supreme Lord."

By following *dharma* in its truest sense, one can attain the highest goal—eternal bliss in the service of the Lord.

CHAPTER 19

THE TOPMOST MEDITATION TECHNIQUE FOR THIS AGE

Introduction to Meditation

Before we discuss what is considered the topmost meditation technique for this age, it's essential to understand what meditation truly is. In simple words, meditation is a practice where an individual uses a method to focus their mind and increase awareness, allowing them to step back from automatic, wandering thoughts. This leads to a clearer mind and a calm, steady emotional state. An apt analogy is that of a pond with still water or a steady, unwavering flame.

Why is it important to cultivate a calm, composed, and still mind, even for just a few minutes each day? Research has shown that to accomplish anything in life, one needs this mental state. In fact, the best decisions in life are made when we are in a peaceful mindset, allowing us to think clearly and make choices based on logic rather than emotions. Moreover, peace of mind, a beneficial outcome of meditation, is highlighted in the Bhagavad Gita, Verse 2.66, which states that there can be no happiness without peace. Common sense tells us that if we cannot be peaceful, how can we be happy? However, as outlined in the Vedas, a peaceful state of mind, effective decision-making, stress reduction, good mental health, and similar benefits are not the ultimate goals of meditation; they are merely by-products. What then is the real goal of meditation? However, before discussing this question, we need to understand the roots of the process of meditation, as envisioned in the Vedic scriptures.

What Exactly is Meditation?

Meditation involves deliberately focusing the mind on a specific object or thought. Automatic forms of meditation occur 24 hours a day—such as the dreams we experience at night. These are influenced by our thoughts during the day. Hundreds and thousands of images, sounds, touches, smells, and tastes are recorded within the mind through sensory inputs, which is why, in dreams, one can smell, taste, touch, see, etc. These recordings are then played back by the mind during moments of leisure. In this context, when we talk about meditation, we refer to the conscious effort to fix our thoughts on a particular object, rather than allowing the mind to wander toward thoughts that provide pleasure or avoid those that cause sorrow. In deliberate meditation, however, the practitioner aims to embrace thoughts related to the object of meditation, while rejecting all other thoughts

Two Types of Meditation

There are two main types of meditation:

1. Form-based Meditation: This involves focusing the mind on a mental image of an object or person.
2. Sound-based Meditation: This technique centres around sound vibrations, often referred to as *mantras*. Sound-based meditation is also known as *Japa*.

Different forms and *mantras* offer varying results and benefits, depending on what the practitioner meditates upon and the intensity of their focus. A common question arises: Should meditation be practised with eyes closed, open, or semi-closed? Meditation with closed eyes can sometimes lead to dozing off, whereas fully open eyes may invite distractions from the surrounding environment. Typically, meditation is practised with semi-closed eyes, providing a balance that minimizes distraction and avoids sleepiness.

The Best Type of Meditation for this Age

In an age characterized by constant distraction, which form of meditation is more suitable: form-based or sound-based? Form-based meditation can be challenging as it requires consistently keeping the mind focused on a particular image, which can lead to interruptions in the meditation process. In the Bhagavad Gita, Arjuna says in Verse 6.34 that controlling the mind is even more difficult than controlling the wind. The mind naturally flickers and constantly shifts from one thought or form to another. The meditation process entails bringing back the distracted mind to the object of meditation.

It is easier to meditate on something tangible rather than on a mental image. For instance, during form-based meditation, external sounds—like a ringing mobile phone—can easily capture our attention, diverting it from the intended object of focus. Hence, sound-based meditation is easier to practise, though the mind is distracted even during this process.

As we discussed earlier, sound-based meditation entails chanting a particular *mantra* and listening to it attentively. Practitioners often use chanting beads, which usually have a count of 108 in Hinduism, though this count may differ in other religions. Unlike form-based meditation, sound-based meditation engages more senses: the fingers handle the beads, the voice is active in chanting, the ears listen, and the mind focuses on the *mantra*. It is essential to chant the *mantra* consciously and to consistently bring the mind back to the specific chant. With technological advancements, numerous powerful distractions have emerged, readily accessible through electronic devices. Consequently, sound-based meditation is increasingly regarded as a better practice in today's world.

Different Objects of Meditation

Teachers in the field of meditation often suggest focusing on a single point, a source of light, an image of their favourite deity, a *mantra,* etc. As stated earlier, depending upon the object of meditation and the intensity of meditation, different results are achieved, ranging from health benefits to spiritual insights. At the very least, one can expect mental health benefits, such as stress relief, mental peace, and relaxation. If the object of meditation is an inert object, like a single point or a flame, as in Trataka or a source of light, the benefits remain confined to health. For instance, in *Pranayama*, focusing on the breath promotes good physical and mental health. However, when the object of meditation involves superior sentient beings who are aware that someone is meditating on them, the benefits can be more significant and are influenced by the satisfaction of the being who is meditated upon. The Vedas include hundreds of *mantras* for invoking the favour of superior deities, also called demigods. If the presiding deities of the *mantras* are appeased, they may bestow desired boons upon the practitioner.

What is a *Mantra*?

A mantra is a specific sound vibration that differs from mere noise. While noise conveys no meaning and lacks structure, a *mantra* possesses purpose and significance. A mantra is a sacred sound or phrase that is considered powerful and special in many spiritual traditions. It can be a single syllable, a word, or a group of words, often in languages like Sanskrit. Some *mantras* have clear meanings and grammatical structure, while others are just sounds without a specific literal meaning.

Mantra Japa and its Types

Mantra japa is the practice of repeating the same *mantra* many times. The most common repetition count is 108, but sometimes people may also repeat it 5, 10, 28, or even 1008 times. *Japa* means the meditative repetition of a *mantra* or a deity's name. This practice is found in Hinduism, Jainism, Sikhism, and Buddhism, and similar practices also exist in other religions. *Japa* can be practised while seated in meditation, during daily activities, or as part of group worship. The *mantra* can be spoken out loud, softly, or silently in the mind. Often, people use a string of prayer beads called a *japamala* to track their repetitions, typically composed of 108 beads made of various materials. Some people wear them around their neck, while others keep them in a cloth bag to keep them clean and private.

Types of *Japa* Based on Loudness

Japa can be performed in several ways, depending on how loudly it is spoken:

1. **Vaikhari Japa:** This involves speaking the *mantra* aloud, loud enough for others nearby to hear. It is particularly

helpful in noisy environments or when focus is difficult and is often recommended for beginners.

2. **Upamshu Japa:** This is done in a whisper, with minimal lip movement. It is considered 100 times more powerful than Vaikhari Japa. It's more subtle and private.
3. **Manasika Japa:** This entails silently repeating the *mantra* in the mind, with no sound or lip movement. It is believed to be 1,000 times more powerful than Upamshu and 100,000 times more powerful than Vaikhari. However, it is hard to perform without first practising the other forms, Vaikhari and Upamshu.

There are several popular and powerful *mantras* mentioned in the Vedas, like Om or Pranava, the Gayatri Mantra, the Pavamana Mantra, the Shanti Mantra, as well as mantras dedicated to deities like Lord Shiva, Devi, Lord Ganesh, Lord Vishnu, and Lord Krishna. In the Bhagavad Gita, Chapter 11, Lord Krishna shows Arjuna His *Virat Rupa*, the Universal Form. In that form, Arjuna sees all the demigods and demigoddesses as different limbs of the form of the Lord. What this means is that just by worshipping Lord Krishna, in a single act, one can worship all the demigods and demigoddesses. The Srimad Bhagavata Purana provides two examples to illustrate this point. The first example is that if one supplies water to the root of the tree, all the parts of the tree benefit from the water. The second example is that when food is given to the stomach, all parts of the body receive nourishment from that food. Another example found in the Vedic scriptures is that just by worshipping the cow, one worships all the different demigods and demigoddesses.

Conclusion

In conclusion, we should focus on one Vedic chant that satisfies all divine personalities. In the Bhagavad Gita Mahatmya, Adi Sankacarya states: "*ekam sastram devaki putra gitam, eko devo devaki putra eva, eko mantrani tasya namani ani karmapy ekam tasya devasya seva*", which means just by reading one book, the Bhagavad Gita, one can makes life successful; by worshipping Lord Krishna, all others are worshipped; by chanting His name, all names are included; and by serving Him, all are served.

The best way to worship Lord Krishna in Kali Yuga is to chant the *Mahamantra* or the Great *Mantra*:

Hare Krishna Hare Krishna
Krishna Krishna Hare Hare,
Hare Rama Hare Rama
Rama Rama Hare Hare.

This Vedic chant is mentioned in the *Kali Santarana Upanishad* as a specific and most powerful *mantra* for mitigating the dangerous effects of Kali Yuga.

CHAPTER 20

ANCIENT VEDIC SCRIPTURES AND THEIR ESSENCE

Introduction

The Vedic tradition is an ocean of divine knowledge—timeless, vast, and profound. Over the millennia, sages and seekers have turned to its sacred scriptures for guidance on how to live with purpose, integrity, and spiritual clarity. Within this enormous body of literature, two texts stand supreme as the distilled essence of Vedic wisdom: the Bhagavad Gita and the Srimad Bhagavatam. These sacred texts are not just philosophical treatises; they are living conversations, revealing the heart of the Vedas and inviting every sincere soul to embark on the journey of self-realization and divine love.

Both the Gita and the Bhagavatam offer more than theoretical knowledge; they present practical, life-transforming insights that illuminate the path of *bhakti*, or loving devotion to the Supreme Personality of Godhead, Sri Krishna. In this chapter, we will explore the origins, structure, and significance of the broader Vedic scriptures and then delve into how these two jewels—the Bhagavad Gita and the Srimad Bhagavatam—serve as their pinnacle, their essence, and their ultimate gift to humanity.

The Vastness of Vedic Knowledge

Vedic knowledge is considered *sanatana dharma*—eternal, universal truths revealed by the Supreme Lord for the upliftment of all living beings. The Vedas are not products of human invention; they are *apaurusheya*, meaning "not created by man". This divine knowledge has been carefully passed down through a chain of disciplic succession (*parampara*) for thousands of years.

The Body of Vedic Literature

1. The Four Vedas (Rig, Yajur, Sama, and Atharva) - These are the original revelations of divine wisdom. They contain hymns, *mantras*, rituals, and metaphysical insights. Their concluding portions, known as the Upanishads, focus on deeper spiritual truths, discussing the eternal nature of the soul (*atman*), the Absolute Truth (*Brahman*), and the illusory nature of material existence.
2. The Itihasas (Ramayana and Mahabharata) - These epic histories, composed in poetic Sanskrit, depict the lives of divine personalities such as Lord Rama and Lord Krishna. They present *dharma* in action and demonstrate how eternal principles apply in the practical world.
3. The Puranas - These eighteen major and eighteen minor texts narrate the cosmic history of creation, the genealogies of demigods and sages, and inspiring stories that embody deep spiritual lessons. The Puranas are meant to make Vedic wisdom accessible to people from all walks of life.
4. The Vedanta Sutras (Brahma Sutras) - Composed by Srila Vyasadeva, these aphorisms systematize Vedic knowledge

into a concise philosophical framework. However, they are cryptic and require commentary to be understood.

Despite this massive and layered corpus, the Vedas ultimately direct us toward one supreme conclusion: the Supreme Personality of Godhead, Sri Krishna, is the ultimate reality, the cause of all causes, and the object of all spiritual endeavour.

The Bhagavad Gita – The Supreme Manual for Life and Liberation

The Bhagavad Gita, spoken by Lord Krishna to Arjuna on the battlefield of Kurukshetra, is one of the most profound philosophical dialogues in human history. Though it appears within the Mahabharata, it is recognized independently as a universal scripture transcending sectarian boundaries.

In just 700 verses, the Gita distills the essence of all Vedic wisdom into a clear and structured path for spiritual elevation. It provides not only a metaphysical understanding of reality, but also a practical framework for living a purposeful, ethical, and spiritually centred life.

Key Teachings of the Bhagavad Gita

1. The Science of the Soul – Lord Krishna establishes that the soul (*jivatma*) is eternal, indestructible, and distinct from the temporary body (2.13, 2.20). The soul undergoes a cycle of birth and death through 8.4 million species, guided by the twin principles of desire and *karma*. Only through spiritual knowledge can one break free from this endless cycle of transmigration (*samsara*).
2. The Three Modes of Material Nature – The Gita categorizes material nature into three modes or *gunas*: goodness (*sattva*), passion (*rajas*), and ignorance (*tamas*)

(14.5–18). These modes bind the soul to different types of behaviour, consciousness, and destinies. One must first elevate oneself to *sattva-guna* and from there transcend all modes to attain the transcendental platform of devotion.

3. Yoga: A Ladder to the Divine – The Gita systematically describes the different forms of yoga: Karma Yoga (selfless action), Jnana Yoga (path of knowledge), and Dhyana Yoga (meditation). However, Krishna emphatically declares that Bhakti Yoga, or devotional service, is the supreme yoga system (6.47, 18.65), for it establishes a loving relationship with the Supreme Person.
4. Surrender to the Lord – The climactic teaching of the Gita is Lord Krishna's merciful instruction to Arjuna: "Abandon all varieties of *dharma* and simply surrender unto Me. I shall deliver you from all sinful reactions. Do not fear." (18.66). This surrender (*sharanagati*) is the key to liberation.

Thus, the Bhagavad Gita serves as both an introduction and gateway to the path of devotion (*bhakti*), making profound truths available in a systematic and engaging manner.

The Srimad Bhagavatam – The Nectar of Devotion

If the Bhagavad Gita is the philosophical foundation, the Srimad Bhagavatam is the emotional and experiential flowering of Vedic wisdom. Compiled by Srila Vyasadeva in his spiritual maturity, the Bhagavatam is the natural commentary on the Vedanta Sutras and the final gift of the Vedic tradition to the world.

It comprises 12 cantos, 335 chapters, and over 18,000 verses, yet its central theme remains consistent: pure, unmotivated devotional service (*ahaituki bhakti*) to Lord Sri Krishna as the highest perfection of life.

Why the Srimad Bhagavatam is the Essence of the Vedas

1. Exclusive Focus on the Supreme Lord – While other Puranas mix topics related to mundane religion, cosmology, and rituals, the Bhagavatam is uniquely centred on Krishna as the Supreme Personality of Godhead (1.1.1). It begins by establishing Krishna as the source of all incarnations and ends by glorifying the holy name as the ultimate means of deliverance in the age of Kali.
2. Unalloyed Devotion as the Goal – The Bhagavatam clearly teaches that the true goal of life is not *dharma, artha, kama*, or even *moksha*, but pure love of God (*prema*): "*Sa vai pumsam paro dharmo yato bhaktir adhokshaje...*" (1.2.6) – Real religion is that which awakens loving service to the Lord.
3. Lord's *lilas* and the Taste of Divine Love – Through enchanting narratives of Krishna's childhood in Vrindavan, His majestic activities in Dwaraka, and His teachings in Hastinapur, the reader is drawn into a world where God is not just worshipped, but also loved as a friend, son, or beloved.
4. The Voices of Saints and Devotees – The Bhagavatam features timeless prayers and realizations from great souls like Prahlada, Dhruva, Ambarisha, Kapila Muni, the *gopis*, and Uddhava. These stories are not mere mythology; they are living expressions of transcendental consciousness.

The Unifying Message: *Bhakti* is Supreme

Together, the Bhagavad Gita and Srimad Bhagavatam offer a complete spiritual path—philosophy and realization, instruction and inspiration. The Gita invites us to surrender to Krishna; the

Bhagavatam shows us the bliss that comes from doing so. The Gita gives us the compass; the Bhagavatam provides us the map and destination.

Conclusion: The Crown Jewels of Vedic Wisdom

The entirety of Vedic literature ultimately converges into one essential truth: Krishna is the Supreme Personality of Godhead, and loving service to Him is the highest perfection of life.

The Bhagavad Gita and Srimad Bhagavatam are not mere texts; they are divine revelations that speak directly to the soul. Those who sincerely study and apply their teachings will not only achieve intellectual clarity but will also experience transformation at the deepest level.

As declared in the Srimad Bhagavatam (1.3.40):

"This Bhagavatam is the essence of all Vedanta philosophy because its subject matter is the Absolute Truth, which, while non-different from the individual soul, is the ultimate goal of life. This scripture is meant for those who are fully pure in heart."

Let the seeker, therefore, take full shelter of these sacred texts, especially as presented by pure devotees like Srila Prabhupada, whose translations and purports of both the Gita and Bhagavatam remain unmatched in authenticity, clarity, and spiritual potency.

By immersing ourselves in their teachings, we take definite steps toward life's ultimate destination—eternal, blissful service to Sri Krishna in the spiritual world.

CHAPTER 21

FROM INSIGHT TO ACTION: A ROADMAP FOR SOULFUL LIVING

As we draw this heartfelt journey to a close, it's time to take a deep breath and reflect on the nourishing ingredients we've stirred into the soul's soup pot. From the nature of the soul and the subtle science of consciousness, to the pursuit of happiness and the profound truths about God, this book has served as an invitation to rediscover your true self and realign your life with timeless wisdom.

However, **knowledge without action is like soup without salt—warm, perhaps, but missing its essence**. If we only read about soup and never drink it, our hunger will remain. In the same way, if we only read about spiritual truths but don't practise them, our soul will stay hungry. Inspiration without implementation is like reading a recipe and never cooking the meal. This final chapter is not just a conclusion; it is your practical blueprint, your daily action plan, your executive summary and soul strategy for a more meaningful, peaceful, and purpose-driven life. It's a guide to help you apply everything you've read into your daily life.

Simple steps. Clear actions. Real results.
Because knowledge is powerful only when we live it.

Sutras from Each Chapter of This Book— A Concentrated Drop of Truth

Chapter 1 - Only pure, non-violent nourishment—both in food and wisdom—can truly heal and uplift the soul. Amidst the noise of information, real spiritual knowledge comes from hearing through an unbroken chain of authentic teachers rooted in divine truth.

Chapter 2 - You are not the body but the immortal soul—conscious, unchanging, and eternal. Human life is the gateway to awaken full spiritual potential and break free from the cycle of birth and death.

Chapter 3 - You are not your job, emotions, or thoughts; your true identity is the eternal soul, distinct from the temporary body and mind. Real self-awareness leads to clarity in purpose, alignment in choices, and the unlocking of your unique spiritual potential.

Chapter 4 - Every living being is driven by the unending quest to seek happiness and avoid suffering. Lasting happiness is not in fleeting pleasures, but in reconnecting with our eternal source, God.

Chapter 5 - The existence of a Supreme Being is not a myth, but a logical necessity. God is the intelligent source behind all design. Knowing that God is not blind faith but the deepest self-realization, is a spark of the divine fire for the soul.

Every action creates a reaction—*karma* is the invisible but unfailing justice system of the universe. By understanding and aligning with this law, we move from victimhood to conscious creators of our destiny.

Chapter 6 – God is both formless light (*Brahman*) and the supreme person (*bhagavan*).

Bhagavan is the original source of *Brahman*—eternal, all-attractive, and complete.

Chapter 7 – God is one and supreme; no soul or Guru can become Him. A true Guru is not God, but His transparent guide to lead us to Him.

Chapter 8 – God is one, the Supreme Source of all; the demigods are His empowered deputies, managing cosmic departments under His authority. By worshipping the Supreme Lord directly, one automatically honours all demigods, just as watering the root nourishes the whole tree.

Chapter 9 – God is not the cause of suffering but our well-wisher who empowers us through karma and choice. He patiently waits for us to turn toward Him, always ready to guide, uplift, and embrace us with love.

Chapters 10 – This world is a divine correctional facility where pain becomes the catalyst for enquiry, purification, and ultimately, liberation. What seems like unfair suffering is actually the unfolding of karma and a divine invitation to transcend, transform, and return to our eternal, joyful identity beyond birth and death.

Chapter 11 - Catastrophes are wake-up calls, reminding us that material life is fragile and temporary. Real success lies not in survival alone, but in aligning our lives with eternal principles and purposeful introspection.

Chapter 12 - Like in the movie *The Matrix*, this material world is an illusion that masks the deeper spiritual reality. The choice is ours—to remain comfortably deluded or courageously awaken to the truth of who we really are.

Chapter 13 - Modern science explores the Multiverse, but Vedic wisdom has long described infinite worlds governed by karma and consciousness. These diverse universes reflect God's unlimited creativity, all meant to help the soul evolve toward love and liberation.

Chapter 14 – Life's highest goal is not wealth, pleasure, or fame but pure love for God, the source of all fulfillments. Without this spiritual direction, even success becomes a disguised failure.

Chapter 15 – Yoga means union; the sacred connection of the soul with the Supreme Lord. Beyond physical postures and breathing, real yoga awakens divine love and eternal consciousness.

Chapter 16 – Among all the different Yoga systems, Bhakti Yoga stands supreme; it transforms the soul through loving service to God. Devotion is the most direct, joyful, and complete means to attain life's ultimate purpose.

Chapter 17 – A genuine Guru is not a middleman, but a transparent medium that connects the soul to God's grace. By hearing from and serving a bona fide spiritual teacher, we accelerate our spiritual growth and avoid misleading detours.

Chapter 18 – *Dharma* is the soul's innate duty to live in alignment with divine truth. Its highest expression is loving devotion to God through *Bhakti*.

Chapter 19 – In this age of relentless distraction, sound-based meditation—especially *mantra japa*—is the most effective means to calm the mind and awaken the soul. Among all mantras, the *Hare Krishna Mahamantra* is declared in the Vedas as the supreme meditation for Kali Yuga, granting both inner peace and ultimate spiritual fulfillment.

Chapter 20 –The Bhagavad Gita and Srimad Bhagavatam are the crown jewels of Vedic wisdom, revealing life's purpose and God's personality. When we study and apply their teachings, we don't just gain knowledge—we taste eternal bliss and inner transformation.

EPILOGUE

A Practical Spiritual Action Plan

Now, let us put this wisdom to work with a clear, step-by-step spiritual lifestyle guide:

Daily Routine

1. **Morning Meditation (10 minutes)**
   Start chanting one round (108 beads) of the *Hare Krishna Mahamantra* daily:
   "*Hare Krishna Hare Krishna Krishna Krishna Hare Hare,*
   Hare Rama Hare Rama Rama Rama Hare Hare"
   This calms the mind, purifies the heart, and reconnects you to God.

2. **Read for 15 Minutes Daily**
   Read the Srimad Bhagavatam or Srila Prabhupada's *Bhagavad Gita As It Is* for at least 15 minutes every day.

3. Read a chapter from *Vegetable Soup for the Soul* every week and mull over the same.
   Let the timeless words guide your thoughts and choices. For any queries on the contents of the book, connect with the author at praneshwardas@gmail.com.

4. **Eat with Awareness**
   Eat *sattvic*, vegetarian food without onion and garlic, which has been offered to God.

5. **Avoid the Four Pillars of Sinful Life**
   Not eating non-vegetarian food;
   No gambling;
   No illicit sex;
   No intoxication (alcohol, tobacco, drugs).
   This purifies the consciousness and aligns you with divine will.

Weekly Goals

1. **Online Spiritual Association**
   Attend at least one online ISKCON *satsang*, Gita session, or *kirtan*.
   Connect with ISKCON devotees and genuine seekers of truth.

2. **Visit Your Local ISKCON Centre**
   Participate in temple programmes—hear, serve, and associate.
   Find your centre at www.iskconcenters.com or use the ISKCON app.

3. **Serve Others**
   Volunteer in some *seva* in the nearest ISKCON Centre—cooking, cleaning, preaching, donation, or digital outreach.
   Spiritual service expands the heart.

Closing Reflections

In the corporate world, we measure success through metrics. In spiritual life, the true metrics are peace of mind, depth of connection, and inner joy. These are not vague ideals—they are measurable experiences that come from consistent, conscious living.

This book was not just a collection of stories or philosophies; it was a call to action, a bowl of soul-stirring soup.

Now, the bowl is in your hands.

So, sip daily. Share freely. Reflect deeply. And remember: Your greatest responsibility is to rediscover who you truly are—and live from that place.

Vegetable soup is served. May it nourish your soul forever.

Scan this QR code to join my WhatsApp community: